T0286767

Can Taiwan Resist a Large-Scale Military Attack by China?

Assessing Strengths and Vulnerabilities in a Potential Conflict

TIMOTHY R. HEATH, SALE LILLY, EUGENIU HAN

Prepared for the Office of the Secretary of Defense
Approved for public release; distribution unlimited

NATIONAL DEFENSE RESEARCH INSTITUTE

For more information on this publication, visit **www.rand.org/t/RRA1658-1**.

About RAND

The RAND Corporation is a research organization that develops solutions to public policy challenges to help make communities throughout the world safer and more secure, healthier and more prosperous. RAND is nonprofit, nonpartisan, and committed to the public interest. To learn more about RAND, visit www.rand.org.

Research Integrity

Our mission to help improve policy and decisionmaking through research and analysis is enabled through our core values of quality and objectivity and our unwavering commitment to the highest level of integrity and ethical behavior. To help ensure our research and analysis are rigorous, objective, and nonpartisan, we subject our research publications to a robust and exacting quality-assurance process; avoid both the appearance and reality of financial and other conflicts of interest through staff training, project screening, and a policy of mandatory disclosure; and pursue transparency in our research engagements through our commitment to the open publication of our research findings and recommendations, disclosure of the source of funding of published research, and policies to ensure intellectual independence. For more information, visit www.rand.org/about/principles.

RAND's publications do not necessarily reflect the opinions of its research clients and sponsors.

Published by the RAND Corporation, Santa Monica, Calif.
© 2023 RAND Corporation
RAND® is a registered trademark.

Library of Congress Cataloging-in-Publication Data is available for this publication.

ISBN: 978-1-9774-0864-8

Cover image by Wang Yu Ching/Office of the President Republic of China (Taiwan).

About This Report

Taiwan remains an important potential flashpoint between China and the United States. Given the geographic distance between the United States and Taiwan and the military challenge of defeating a major attack by China, an accurate assessment of Taiwan's ability to sustain a defense can be a critical factor for U.S. decisionmakers and planners. In this report, the authors develop a framework for assessing a country's capacity to resist a large-scale military attack. They then use that framework to assess Taiwan's capacity to resist an attack by China for 90 days—the amount of time plausibly required for the United States to marshal sufficient forces to carry out an intervention in East Asia.

The research reported here was initially completed in October 2017. The report was updated in June 2023 and underwent security review with the sponsor and the Defense Office of Prepublication and Security Review before public release.

RAND National Security Research Division

This research was sponsored by the Office of the Secretary of Defense and conducted within the International Security and Defense Policy Program of the RAND National Security Research Division (NSRD), which operates the National Defense Research Institute (NDRI), a federally funded research and development center sponsored by the Office of the Secretary of Defense, the Joint Staff, the Unified Combatant Commands, the Navy, the Marine Corps, the defense agencies, and the defense intelligence enterprise.

For more information on the RAND International Security and Defense Policy Program, see www.rand.org/nsrd/isdp or contact the director (contact information is provided on the webpage).

Acknowledgments

The authors would like to thank Kristen Gunness and Sina Beaghley for reviewing an earlier draft of this document.

Summary

The vast expanse of the Pacific Ocean imposes a formidable obstacle to any attempt by the United States to intervene in a contingency in East Asia, such as one involving Taiwan (officially, the Republic of China). Marshaling and conveying a large expeditionary force across the ocean could take weeks or months. The military challenge of defeating a major attack from China (officially, the People's Republic of China) off its coast also remains formidable, especially given the People's Liberation Army's substantial improvements in its anti-access, area denial capabilities. Accurately assessing Taiwan's ability to sustain a resolute defense against a large-scale military attack for at least three months after the onset of a major assault from China could help U.S. decisionmakers and planners better anticipate and respond in such a situation.

For decades, media commentators have debated how long Taiwan could fend off a Chinese attack. In recent years, the academic community has contributed to the discussion by publishing research on some of the most important factors that appear to correlate with a military's will to fight. This study draws from that literature and from insights gained through interviews with officials and experts in Taiwan and the United States to posit a framework for analyzing and assessing Taiwan's capacity to resist a large-scale attack. In this study, we define *Taiwan's capacity to resist a large-scale attack* as the national government's ability to oversee a resolute defense of the island during a 90-day period from the onset of a major attack by China. We envision that such a major attack will involve a conventional missile attack, a joint blockade campaign, an amphibious invasion, extensive information operations, or some combination of those approaches.

In this analysis, we examine four variables (and related indicators) that are essential to infusing a country with a strong capacity to resist an attack: political leadership and social cohesion, military effectiveness, durability (i.e., a country's ability to sustain and manage the economic and human costs of war), and military intervention by an ally. Strong political leadership (in the form of respected national leaders capable of commanding and enforcing the public's loyalty), a largely unified and cohesive public, and strong public support for a compelling national cause or ideology offer the most essential foundation for a resolute defense. A prepared and capable military can bolster the effects of political leadership by denying the adversary an easy conquest. By staving off imminent defeat, Taiwan's military could prolong the conflict and allow time for foreign intervention to arrive and potentially for international sympathy to develop. Severe disruption to the economy and infrastructure of the island—along with mounting civilian and military casualties—may bolster public resolve in the initial phases of the conflict, but, over the longer term, those disruptions are likely to erode public support for the war. The promise of U.S. intervention offers an additional important resource for infusing determination and resolve, but the effects of promised intervention will depend both on the state of the island's political leadership and military capabilities and on the nature and scope of promised U.S. aid. In general, the weaker that Taiwan's political leadership and its military are, the earlier and more robust the U.S. intervention must be to maximize the prospect that Taiwan will avoid defeat.

Implications

Our findings about Taiwan's capacity to resist a large-scale attack by China raise several implications for U.S. planners and policymakers. First, for insight into Taiwan's capacity, analysts should pay close attention to the quality and strength of Taiwan's political leadership and the degree of social cohesion in the lead-up to a crisis or conflict. The state of the island's military and its enduring economic and infrastructure vulnerabilities should be regarded as of secondary importance.

Second, even though Taiwan has fewer armaments and troops than China does, that does not doom the island to defeat. Taiwan can take important steps to improve the effectiveness of its military. However, even if Taiwan's military dramatically improves its combat-effectiveness, China's military advantage will likely continue to grow because of China's enormous resource advantage. Given these trends, Taiwan's ability to withstand a major attack by China for the posited 90-day period increasingly will hinge on the strength of its political leadership and social cohesion above all other variables.

Third, the impact of severe casualties and economic loss likely would cut two ways in a major war. Initially, Taiwan's public probably would rally around the national leadership and favor resisting an aggressive China. However, over the long term, heavy costs of conflict likely would erode public support for continuing the war. How public support ultimately changes over time could vary depending on the strength of Taiwan's political leaders and the degree of social cohesion.

Finally, because of Taiwan's military disadvantages and low durability, successfully withstanding a large-scale Chinese attack would require military intervention by the United States. A well-led and socially cohesive Taiwan might be able to mount a determined resistance for a long time, but, without a robust U.S. military intervention, China's enormous advantage in military resources likely would allow it to eventually subjugate the island.

Recommendations

U.S. officials should continue to help Taiwan strengthen its military. Improvements in the quality of platforms and weapons, the skill of the troops, the integration of the force, and the military's professional autonomy could increase the lethality of the force and thereby both bolster the island's confidence in its defenses and help deter China. However, China's deepening military advantage suggests that, even with major improvements to Taiwan's defenses, U.S. intervention will remain necessary to deter or defeat a Chinese attack.

U.S. officials can help Taiwan counter Chinese information operations and economic coercion. Chinese authorities have frequently employed such methods as a low-risk way to advance the country's goals, but these tactics have thus far been met with little success in Taiwan. Taiwan is generally better positioned to counter these non-war tactics, but U.S. support in such efforts will remain important.

Finally, even if Taiwan's political leadership and social cohesion are strong and its military is expected to be effective against China's military, U.S. military intervention would be required for Taiwan to withstand a major attack. The speed, clarity, and credibility of any pledged U.S. military support could be a critical factor in sustaining Taiwan's ability to resist.

Contents

Figures and Tables

Figures

Tables

CHAPTER ONE

Introduction

A growing imbalance between the military forces of the People's Republic of China and Taiwan (officially, the Republic of China) has raised doubts among military experts and political analysts about Taiwan's ability to repel a large-scale attack.[1] Although the United States maintains an implicit security guarantee with Taiwan, military intervention against China poses formidable obstacles. Politically, the grim prospect of major war against a powerful adversary like China raises the likelihood that any potential military intervention would face intense scrutiny and skepticism by U.S. leaders and the public. Washington and the U.S. public might opt against intervention if Taiwan's military rapidly collapsed or if the conflict appeared to be a lost cause. Conversely, a resolute and dogged Taiwanese defense could garner international sympathy and increase the likelihood of U.S. government and public support for opposing Chinese aggression. Because the Pacific Ocean is so vast, it could require considerable time—at least several months—for the United States to mobilize sufficient U.S.-based combat power to augment forward-deployed military forces and fight a major contingency in East Asia. Therefore, for U.S. decisionmakers and planners who might need to respond to a Chinese attack on Taiwan, an accurate judgment of the island's capacity to withstand an attack remains important.

Expert opinion remains divided on how long the people of Taiwan might endure a large-scale attack by China. Military analysts who focus on the quantity and quality of forces available to fight a war have generally offered skeptical assessments. For example, an analysis published in 2014 judged that the ships, aircraft, and weapons available to Taiwan to counter a Chi-

---

[1] For simplicity, in this report, we use *China* to refer to the People's Republic of China and *Taiwan* to refer to the Republic of China.

nese attack were inadequate.[2] Similarly, a 2022 U.S. Department of Defense report to Congress outlined scenarios in which Chinese military forces could employ a blockade, firepower strikes, or an invasion to subjugate the island, suggesting that the island remained deeply vulnerable.[3]

On the other hand, analysts who focus on Taiwan's politics have offered starkly contrasting assessments of the island's potential resolve in war. Official Chinese news sources have derisively dismissed Taiwan's service members as fragile "strawberry troops" [草莓兵] who would crumble in the first moments of battle.[4] These Chinese sources appear to base their views on observations that Taiwan's conscript forces are poorly prepared. However, other observers have concluded that Taiwan's political will to fight may be greatly underestimated. As an example, one commentator has pointed out that a Chinese attack would likely rally the Taiwan populace. The commentator cited numerous historical precedents in which people have tended to "resist, rather than surrender" when coerced or attacked.[5]

Whether Taiwan has the military and political capacity to resist an attack remains highly debatable even among the island's leadership. In 2014, Taiwan Defense Minister Yen Ming stated that, if China launched a full-scale attack, Taiwan would "last at least one month" without help from the United States.[6] However, the comment spurred National Security Bureau Chief Tsai Der-sheng to suggest that even one month may be too long. Tsai stated, "whether the nation is capable of holding out for a month also depends on the public's will to resist an invasion. If everyone wants to leave,

---

[2] Kyle Mizokami, "How Taiwan Would Defend Against a Chinese Attack," USNI News, March 26, 2014.

[3] Office of the Secretary of Defense, *Annual Report to Congress: Military and Security Developments Involving the People's Republic of China 2022*, Washington, D.C.: U.S. Department of Defense, November 29, 2022.

[4] See, for example, Xinhua, "台湾新兵娇生惯养体能训练标准被迫一降再降" ["Training Standards for Spoiled Taiwan Recruits Decline Again and Again"], March 23, 2007.

[5] Michael Thim, "Can China Take Over Taiwan by Force?" *Thinking Taiwan*, January 21, 2015.

[6] Shih Hsiu-chuan, "Taiwan Could Withstand Attack for One Month: Yen," *Taipei Times*, March 7, 2014.

we may not be able to hold out for a month."[7] Adding to the pessimism, Taiwan's defense ministry also predicted in 2013 that China could successfully repel a U.S. intervention and invade the island by 2020.[8]

Part of the difficulty of assessing Taiwan's capacity to resist a large-scale attack lies in the ambiguity and complexity of defining a country's *capacity to fight* (or *will to fight*). The term may refer to either the physical resources available to fend off attack or the intangible political and spiritual resources that underpin the resolve of a country's national leadership, its people, or both. Military experts typically focus on the former, while political analysts typically focus on the latter. And even when analysts employ an assessment approach that accounts for both tangible and intangible dimensions, that approach carries its own complexities and layers of meaning. For example, a country's capacity to fight may encompass a people's tangible and intangible resources to persist in armed conflict during *and after* the national leadership has surrendered—for example, through insurgencies. Moreover, the capacity to resist may vary over time and among parts of the population, and it might depend on the nature of the conflict. That is, a populace that is mobilized to fight furiously early in a war may eventually tire of the hardships and seek peace. And, in some countries, particular ethnic or religious populations might have greater incentives to fight an adversary than other groups do. Finally, the nature of the conflict may spur different reactions as well: People may be willing to endure war when the costs are bearable but balk when war carries the risk of nuclear annihilation. Any analysis of Taiwan's capacity to resist a large-scale attack must therefore specify the principal concepts of interest before drawing conclusions.

---

[7] Rich Chang, Lo Tien-pin, and Jake Chung, "Taiwan Would Not Survive Month of Attack, NSB Says," *Taipei Times*, March 11, 2014.

[8] Michael Gold and Ben Blanchard, "Taiwan Says China Could Launch Successful Invasion by 2020," Reuters, October 9, 2013.

Research Approach

In this report, we seek to assess Taiwan's capacity to resist a large-scale attack by China. To do so, we focus on the national leadership and the early period of conflict, when U.S. decisionmakers may have an opportunity to direct a military intervention. We seek to discern the most-important tangible and intangible factors that contribute to a country's capacity to sustain resistance to an attack. In particular, we examine the role of Taiwan's political leadership and social cohesion, the military's effectiveness, and vulnerabilities in the economy and infrastructure. We also examine factors that could influence an assessment, such as the scope and duration of the attack and the scope and scale of economic coercion. Finally, we assess the impact that a promised intervention by the U.S. military might have on Taiwan's willingness to keep fighting.

In this report, we define *Taiwan's capacity to resist a large-scale attack* as the national government's ability to oversee a resolute military defense of the island during a 90-day period from the onset of a major attack by China. We envision that such an attack will involve a conventional missile attack, a joint blockade campaign, an amphibious invasion, extensive information operations, or some combination of those approaches. This definition focuses on the national government as the principal agent making decisions about the military and whether to sustain or abandon the war effort. This focus on the government also acknowledges the critical importance of public sentiment, because national leaders who lack popular support will struggle to maintain a war footing. However, we seek to measure the impact of popular support indirectly, by analyzing the social cohesion and the level of popular support for the government in Taiwan. In this study, we also eschew questions about Taiwan's potential to maintain insurgencies in the event of surrender by national authorities. Because we seek to inform U.S. planning and decisionmaking in a conflict scenario, analyzing the capacity for insurgencies is beyond the purview of this study. Instead, we focus on a 90-day period from the onset of hostilities as a minimum time that U.S. forces would need to mobilize forces for an intervention in East Asia.

In addition, in this report, we examine only the most-stressing scenarios involving a Chinese large-scale attack designed to compel unification or otherwise compel Taiwan to accept Beijing's sovereignty over it. The military

4

operation under consideration may include any combination of a conventional missile attack, a joint blockade campaign, an amphibious invasion, or extensive information operations. We define a successful Taiwan defense as follows: The national government must remain in power throughout the 90-day period. As the governing authority, it must be able to carry out basic government functions and be able to reliably communicate and coordinate any U.S. intervention. Furthermore, Taiwan's military must remain capable of denying China the ability to remove the Taiwanese government from power or otherwise compel Taiwan's leadership to surrender on whatever terms Beijing demands. However, for a successful defense, Taiwan does not need to win every battle, or even most of them. For the purposes of the study, Taiwan's military must merely remain cohesive and continue fighting while the national government remains in power.

Small-scale Chinese coercive operations to extract relatively minor concessions or punish Taiwan for perceived intransigence—such as demonstrations, missile tests, exercises, or even limited strikes—do not test the country's capacity to resist in a significant manner and are not reviewed in this study. However, as part of our assessment of the island's ability to withstand the costs of war, we analyze potential Chinese economic sanctions and Taiwan's options to counter them (see Appendixes A–C).

Data and Methodology

To perform this analysis, we collected information from social science literature, historical case studies, open-source reporting, and interviews with individuals and experts in the United States and Taiwan. Particularly valuable among the social science literature were studies of national cohesion in wartime and military effectiveness. Studies of historical experiences with blockades and military coercion also proved useful. In addition, we reviewed publicly available data regarding Taiwan's politics, polls, state of military readiness, economy, and infrastructure. These sources are reviewed in more detail in Chapter Two. To supplement the analysis of social science literature and open-source documents, we also interviewed former U.S. government officials responsible for policy on Taiwan, as well as experts, officials, political leaders, and activists in Taiwan.[9] These sources provided background information and valuable insights, but we do not specifically use information from the interviews in this report; thus, they are not cited in the text.

Organization of This Report

The report proceeds as follows. Chapter Two describes a basic theoretical model for assessing a country's capacity to resist a large-scale attack. The model draws from historical case studies and contemporary scholarship, and we use it to argue that a country's capacity to resist a large-scale attack depends on four key variables:

1. the country's political leadership and social cohesion
2. the effectiveness of the country's military
3. the country's ability to sustain and manage the economic and human costs of war (i.e., the country's durability)
4. military intervention by an ally.

In that chapter, we also propose measurements that can help an analyst evaluate each of these variables and score them as part of a comprehensive assessment.

In Chapter Three, we apply this theoretical model to Taiwan. Although it is impossible to predict how Taiwan will behave in a crisis or conflict, especially given how each variable could change depending on the context, the assessment can provide a sense of major vulnerabilities and can identify key indicators that bear monitoring for insight into how Taiwan's national leaders might act in a conflict.

In Chapter Four, we examine how Taiwan's capacity to resist a large-scale attack might evolve during an intensifying cross-Strait crisis or conflict. A hypothetical scenario involving conflict between China and Taiwan is sufficiently different from the current situation that predicting its evolu-

---

[9] The study was reviewed by RAND's Human Subjects Protection Committee and was determined not to be human subjects research.

tion is difficult under the best of circumstances, owing to the influence of unforeseen and unanticipated variables.

Chapter Five concludes the report and identifies the implications of this research for U.S. planners and decisionmakers.

The appendixes provide analysis of Taiwan's economic dependence on China, possible tools of Chinese economic coercion, and options that could enable Taiwan to withstand such coercion.

CHAPTER TWO

Key Variables for a Country's Capacity to Resist an Attack

Interest in studying a country's capacity to resist a large-scale attack, or the country's "will to fight," has expanded in recent years, yielding a large and growing body of scholarship. However, the academic community has not reached consensus on any generalized theory on the topic. At most, the academic research and historical case studies have provided some insight into the most-important factors that contribute to a military's will to fight. This literature is reviewed in detail in subsequent sections of this chapter, but we first summarize the main findings.

In determining the resolve of a country (which, in this report and elsewhere, includes the government, people, and military) to fight a war, the most important variable is the country's *political leadership and social cohesion*.[1] The *military's effectiveness* plays a key role as well, of course. To sustain a national will to fight, a country's military must have some hope of securing victory or at least denying victory for the adversary.[2] The military may be inferior in quantity and quality, but the disadvantage should not be so overwhelming that the prospects of victory seem impossible. A third variable that determines a nation's resolve to fight is its *durability*—that is, its ability to sustain and manage the economic and human costs of conflict.[3]

---

[1] Jasen J. Castillo, *Endurance and War: The National Sources of Military Cohesion*, Stanford, Calif.: Stanford University Press, 2014.

[2] Paul K. Huth, *Standing Your Ground: Territorial Disputes and International Conflict*, Ann Arbor, Mich.: University of Michigan, 1998, p. 114.

[3] Robert A. Pape, *Bombing to Win: Air Power and Coercion in War*, Ithaca, N.Y.: Cornell University Press, 1996, p. 10.

Often, high costs at the onset of a conflict can steel a nation's resolve; however, these costs may erode support over the longer term. Finally, *military intervention by an ally* may affect a country's resolve. Although few studies have examined this variable, available evidence suggests that the impact may be influenced by how the conflict began, the speed with which the ally intervenes, and the robustness of the commitment. Figure 2.1 depicts how these variables influence a country's ability to resist attack.

In the rest of this chapter, we provide an overview of each of the four variables assessed in this study as essential to infusing a country with a strong capacity to fight:

- political leadership and social cohesion
- military effectiveness
- durability
- military intervention by an ally (as necessary).

FIGURE 2.1

Key Variables in a Country's Ability to Resist an Attack

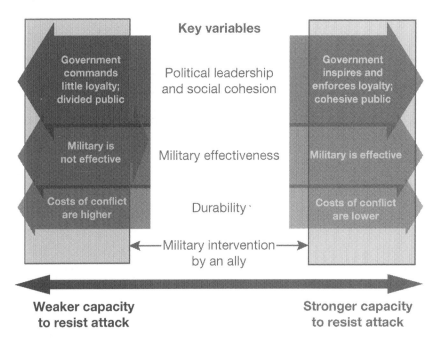

SOURCE: Authors' analysis informed by Castillo, 2014; Huth, 1998; Pape, 1996.

Each section also includes a discussion of indicators for measuring each variable. To provide a sense of the relative importance of each variable, we assigned numerical values to these indicators. For two variables (military effectiveness and durability), the related indicators were assigned a value of 1 for a score that we identify as *low* and 2 for a score that we identify as *high*. For reasons that are explained in more detail later, the indicators for the other two variables—(1) political leadership and social cohesion and (2) military intervention by an ally—were assigned a low score of 1, a medium score of 2, and a high score of 3. These number values are provided only to give analysts a sense of the relative importance of various indicators when carrying out a comprehensive assessment and should not be viewed as a mathematical means of calculating and predicting outcomes. In addition, throughout this chapter, we describe how we measure each indicator in our framework; other analysts using this framework to conduct a similar assessment might choose to measure the indicators using different definitions for low and high scores.

Variable 1: Political Leadership and Social Cohesion

Numerous studies have established the importance of strong political leadership and social cohesion for waging war in a resolute and tenacious manner. In a 2014 report, Jasen Castillo, a professor at Texas A&M, concluded that strong political leadership provides the most essential foundation for a robust national will to fight.[4] Similarly, in a study for the Strategic Studies Institute, M. Chris Mason found that "a strong and stable government and a strong and stable society are the essential precursors, the *sine qua non*, for a strong army. If they don't exist, there cannot be a strong army: if there is no nation to fight for, no national army will fight for it."[5] Senior U.S. military leaders arrived at similar conclusions as early as 1954, when the Joint Chiefs of Staff warned Secretary of State John Foster Dulles that

---

[4] Castillo, 2014.

[5] M. Chris Mason, "Strategic Insights: The Will to Fight," Strategic Studies Institute, U.S. Army War College, September 11, 2015.

"strong and stable governments and societies are necessary to support the creation of strong armies."[6]

Countries with national leaders and governments capable of inspiring intense loyalty and demanding great sacrifice in service of a messianic ideology have often prevailed over their adversaries despite repeated battlefield setbacks and enormous costs in blood and treasure. In World War II, for example, Soviet leader Joseph Stalin upheld an ideology of revolutionary communism and wielded dictatorial powers to enforce loyalty and brutally punish disloyalty. Despite an initially weak military performance, widespread devastation, and catastrophic military and civilian casualties numbering in the millions, the Soviet military fought doggedly and eventually defeated the Nazi invaders.[7] Similarly, intense devotion to messianic ideologies and strong political leaders has infused insurgent movements throughout history with a fervent fighting spirit. The victories of national liberationist movements in Algeria in the 1950s, Indochina in the 1960s, and Afghanistan in the 1980s underscore the importance of political leadership and ideology in infusing militaries with a relentless will to fight.

In addition, legitimacy and strong, popular leadership are important influences. In World War II, for example, the Franklin D. Roosevelt administration and the war against fascism enjoyed wide support in the United States: Public approval ratings of the President averaged 65 percent from 1937 to 1943.[8] And the U.S. military performed effectively throughout the war. Moreover, a public's support for the nation's leadership in times of conflict is likely to be strongly influenced by the opinion of elites (i.e., the social groups in a society who have higher levels of wealth, skills, and education). Research by Adam Berinsky, a scholar at the Massachusetts Institute of Technology, indicates that the public's view of how national leaders are prosecuting a war is strongly influenced by the presence or absence of conflict among such elites. When the elites are relatively unified, the public tends to

---

[6] Ronald H. Spector, *Advice and Support: The Early Years, 1941–1960*, Stockton, Calif.: University Press of the Pacific, 2005, p. 379.

[7] J. T. Dykman, "The Soviet Experience in World War II," Eisenhower Institute at Gettysburg College, undated.

[8] Matthew A. Baum and Samuel Kernell, "Economic Class and Popular Support for Franklin Roosevelt in War and Peace," *Public Opinion Quarterly*, Vol. 65, No. 2, 2001.

support the war. When elites are divided, however, mass support declines. Thus, if the public and elites withdraw political support, national leaders might not be able to sustain the war effort.[9]

Public support for a country's leaders may differ in times of peace and war, but extremely low levels of peacetime support can impair efforts to build wartime support. Studies show that elites tend to be unified in support of a nation's goals during an international crisis and in the early phases of a war, which has correlated with high public approval ratings for national leaders during a crisis.[10] However, low approval ratings of a nation's leaders during peacetime could affect public support for a war conducted by the same leaders over the medium to long term.[11] For example, polls taken in 2003, during the first year of the war in Iraq, indicated that more than 70 percent of Americans initially approved of the government's handling of the conflict. But negative public perceptions of the George W. Bush administration that preceded the conflict contributed to a steady decline in support for the war. By 2008, less than 40 percent of Americans supported the war, which added immense pressure on the government to scale back U.S. involvement in the conflict.[12]

In contrast, when a government is perceived as illegitimate or its leaders lack popular support, the military may prove unreliable or may even refuse to fight. In the 1940s, Nationalist China suffered severe problems of corruption, abuse, and misgovernment. The unpopularity of the government and its predatory policies sapped the morale of Nationalist armies, which often performed poorly against the Japanese and their domestic Communist rivals. In the cases of French involvement in Algeria and Indochina in the 1950s, the U.S.-backed government in South Vietnam in the 1960s, and

---

[9] Adam J. Berinsky, "Assuming the Costs of War: Events, Elites, and American Public Support for Military Conflict," *Journal of Politics*, Vol. 69, No. 4, November 2007.

[10] W. Lance Bennett and David L. Paletz, eds., *Taken by Storm: The Media, Public Opinion, and U.S. Foreign Policy in the Gulf War*, Chicago, Ill.: University of Chicago Press, 1994, pp. 12–42.

[11] Adam J. Berinsky and James N. Druckman, "Public Opinion Research and Support for the Iraq War," *Public Opinion Quarterly*, Vol. 71, No. 1, Spring 2007.

[12] Pew Research Center, "Public Attitudes Toward the War in Iraq: 2003–2008," March 19, 2008.

the Soviet-backed government in Afghanistan, governments that enjoyed qualitatively superior weaponry and the support of the technologically advanced, lethal militaries of their Western backers fell to militarily inferior opponents. In each case, problems of weak leadership and lack of legitimacy for the national government sapped the fighting spirit and resolve of their respective armed forces.

In wartime, many individuals may be reluctant to sacrifice themselves to the cause outlined by national authorities. The ability of national governments to enforce loyalty and punish defection can help instill discipline and deter troops from desertion. This ability may be especially important in times of military setbacks. The ability of authoritarian regimes to punish disloyalty, as Nazi Germany did in the waning days of World War II, can incentivize troops to stay in the field and keep fighting even as the prospects of victory dim. Although frequently controversial, liberal democracies have sometimes employed restrictions to control opposition to war, as the United States and many Western European countries did during World War I and World War II. And, during the Civil War, U.S. President Abraham Lincoln resorted to controversial measures to control political opposition and sustain the nation's resolve against the Confederacy.[13]

Furthermore, countries with a high degree of ethnic, sectarian, or political polarization and division have had difficulty sustaining cohesion in combat. Militaries reflect the social, political, and ethnic makeup of the broader society from which troops are recruited. Therefore, a society characterized by a high degree of cohesion is far more likely to have a unified military, while social or ethnic divisions can impair motivation. A 1996 book by Stephen Peter Rosen, a prominent military theorist at Harvard University, noted that divisions along ethnic and class lines have weakened the effectiveness of India's military.[14] In another example, in 1940, France enjoyed a modern, industrialized economy and a liberal democratic government. However, it also had a highly polarized society and a divided, weak leadership that reflect the country's social and class divisions. Despite possessing technologically superior tanks and weapons in many cases and larger

---

[13] Castillo, 2014.

[14] Stephen Peter Rosen, *Societies and Military Power: India and Its Armies*, Ithaca, N.Y.: Cornell University Press, 1996.

numbers of tanks and artillery than their German adversaries, many French units quickly collapsed in combat during World War II, partly because of the deleterious effects of paralyzing political and social divisions.[15] And, in recent years, U.S. efforts to equip newly established national militaries in Iraq and Afghanistan with advanced weapons and technologies have failed to overcome the persistent weaknesses posed by deep sectarian divides. On May 24, 2015, referring to the Iraqi Army created by the United States following the execution of Saddam Hussein, then–Secretary of Defense Ashton Carter said, "We can give them training, we can give them equipment—we obviously can't give them the will to fight."[16]

In summary, having strong political leadership and social cohesion is essential to ensuring a country's determination to fight. We consider a country to be strong in this variable if the national government and political leaders have relatively unified public support, the ability to inspire intense loyalty in service of a self-sacrificing cause or ideology or to enforce loyalty in wartime, a cohesive society, and a compelling ideology. Next, we propose a series of indicators to help assess the quality of a country's political leadership and social cohesion.

Indicators of Political Leadership and Social Cohesion

Four indicators provide a means of measuring a country's political leadership and social cohesion. Table 2.1 summarizes each one and how we measure it. Because we assess that this variable is the biggest contributor to a nation's capacity and resolve to resist a large-scale attack, the related indicators are weighted higher than the indicators for some other variables. For this variable's indicators, a low score equals 1, and a high score equals 3; there is no score of 2.

The first indicator for this variable is *public support for the national leadership*. As noted previously, research on past wars suggests that national leaders are better positioned to carry out a war if they enjoy broad public support. In this study, we measure this indicator using public opinion polls.

---

[15] Castillo, 2014.

[16] Barbara Starr, "Carter: Iraqis Showed 'No Will to Fight' in Ramadi," CNN, May 24, 2015.

TABLE 2.1

Indicators of Political Leadership and Social Cohesion

Indicator	Explanation	Measurement (high score = 3)
Public support for the national leadership	High levels of popular and elite support enable national leaders to prosecute war more freely.	How strong is the government's support? High score = In peacetime, popular polls show that more people support than oppose the leadership; in wartime, a large majority support the leadership.
Ability of the national government to enforce loyalty	A government able to enforce loyalty can compel military troops to keep fighting and help restrain desertion.	How effectively can the government enforce loyalty and control social division in wartime? High score = In a war, the government effectively controls organized opposition to war. This indicator is not measured in peacetime.
Cohesiveness of the polity	A cohesive, unified polity is more likely to fight with resolve.	How cohesive or divided is the society? High score = A large majority of the most-salient social, ethnic, or religious groups express trust or favorable views of other groups.
Compelling ideology	An ideology of collective ideals can encourage the mobilization of popular support and increase the motivation of troops.	Is there a network of social relationships in support of an ideology? Is there evidence of the military's commitment to the ideology? High score = There is a clear social network linking political activists, national leaders, and the military, and there are signs that the military embraces the ideology.

Because of the possibilities of political change, assessments during peacetime do not predict wartime performance but may give a sense of potential vulnerabilities. When reviewing polls taken during peacetime, we assign a low score for the public support indicator if more of the public disapproves than approves of the national leadership, and we assign a high score if the polls indicate that more people approve than disapprove. And because past research has identified patterns of relative public unity and strong support during wartime, we believe that a high score in such cases should require a higher threshold of public support. Thus, when reviewing polls taken during wartime, we assign a low score for this indicator if less than a large majority (e.g., 60 percent) of the public disapproves of the national leadership. And we assess a high score if polls show that more than a large majority approves of the national leadership's handling of the war.

The second indicator is the *ability of the national government to enforce loyalty*. There is no evidence to suggest that a government's adoption of censorship, political control, and similar repressive features in peacetime will give it any strategic advantage. Thus, there is no peacetime variant of this indicator; it is relevant only in wartime. We measure this indicator by assessing the government's willingness or ability to suppress significant, organized political opposition to the war. Enforcing loyalty may anger citizens and mask disaffection, and it may not be desirable for some governments that choose to uphold individual liberties even in conflict. However, academic studies of past wars have concluded that such enforcement can contribute significantly to reducing desertion rates in the military and compelling troops to stay in the field, despite battlefield setbacks.[17] For this indicator, we assign a low score if we assess that the government is incapable or unwilling to suppress organized groups that can credibly impede the war effort by encouraging desertion, conducting sabotage, gaining national press coverage for acts of intense opposition to the war, or advocating the adversary's war aims. We assign a high score if the government consistently and effectively controls such groups or if there is little sign of serious organized opposition to the conflict.

The third indicator is the *cohesiveness of the polity*. We measure this indicator by assessing the relative levels of conflict or distrust between different social groups. For democratic countries, we assign a low score if polls suggest strong support for competing parties at the extremes of a spectrum and little support for centrist tendencies in existing parties. For all countries, a low score may be assigned if polls suggest high levels of dislike or distrust between different ethnic, religious, or social groups. We assign a high value if the distribution of popular support in a democracy favors political parties with centrist tendencies or if different ethnic, religious, or social groups show low levels of dislike and distrust. We can measure this indicator through polls that show whether a large majority of members (e.g., more than 60 percent) of the most-salient ethnic, social, or religious groups express strong distrust or other hostile sentiments toward other groups.

---

[17] Castillo, 2014, p. 43.

The fourth indicator is the presence of a *compelling ideology* that influences cohesion and motivation in the military and encourages the mobilization of popular support for war. Scholars have documented that ideology contributes to support for armed groups through the buildup of networks linking political activists, the broader public, leaders, and armed forces.[18] Thus, to measure this indicator, we assess whether there is a network of social relationships among relevant political activists, national leaders, and the military. Evidence of the military's commitment to an ideology may be seen in the form of statements or other official gestures by top leaders in support of the ideology, requirements that military members pledge loyalty to the ideology's aims, or the military's adoption of symbols and insignia of the relevant ideology. For this indicator, we assign a low score if (1) we cannot identify a network of social relationships linking political activists, national leaders, and the military to some political ideology and (2) there is little evidence of commitment to the ideology in the military. We assign a high score if we can identify such a network and if there is clear evidence of the military's commitment to the ideology.

The state of a country's political leadership and social cohesion is an important variable in the capacity to fight a large-scale conflict. We assess this variable as *low* overall if the total of the individual indicators is between 4 and 6, as *medium* if the total is between 7 and 9, and as *high* if the total is between 10 and 12. These values are likely to be more meaningful and easier to assess with confidence during wartime. An evaluation of the same indicators during peacetime can provide only a general assessment that may not apply in war. Indeed, of all the indicators examined in this study, those associated with political leadership and social cohesion are the most prone to dramatic changes between peacetime and conflict. This is because how and why a conflict begins can significantly affect leaders' resolve and the population's cohesiveness. Because we cannot predict what the circumstances will be in the lead-up to a conflict, it is extremely difficult to estimate how peacetime values will change in wartime. Moreover, one of the indicators has no peacetime counterpart. Thus, peacetime assessments of these indicators should be regarded as merely rough and imprecise estimates.

---

[18] Stephano Costalli and Andrea Ruggeri, "Indignation, Ideologies, and Armed Mobilization: Civil War in Italy, 1943–45," *International Security*, Vol. 40, No. 2, Fall 2015.

Variable 2: Military Effectiveness

A capable military can bolster the hopes of a country's people and political leaders during war. As long as a besieged country possesses sufficient quantities of materiel to wage war and the adversary does not possess an overwhelming advantage, the numerically inferior side has reason to believe that it can win a conflict or at least avoid outright defeat. Indeed, research by nationally renowned military expert Stephen Biddle, a professor at George Washington University, shows that militaries with fewer and less-skilled forces historically have shown an equal chance of prevailing against their militarily superior adversaries.[19] In this conceptual model, to estimate the overall strength and effectiveness of a military, we focus on the interplay between two factors: a country's stock of military resources and how well it can translate those resources into combat power.

We can assess a country's stock of military resources by examining the quantity of forces available and the overall quality of the military's weapons, armaments, and equipment. However, such assessments provide only a starting point for estimating a military's effectiveness.

Personnel and organizations play a critical role in translating materiel into combat power. Considerable evidence underscores the importance of education and training for superior combat performance. Technologically advanced militaries depend on an infrastructure of managerial and administrative organizations to ensure the recruitment and preparation of the skilled troops needed to operate highly complex machines in accordance with sophisticated doctrines. Public and private-sector scientists, technicians, and laboratories create and refine the technologies and maintenance and support systems needed to enable smooth and reliable operation of battlefield forces. In particular, the integration of relevant bureaucracies, procedures, and processes ensures that resources can be efficiently converted into combat power. Finally, militaries with more-stable civil-military relations that enable some degree of professional autonomy also tend to demonstrate greater adaptability on the battlefield than heavily politicized forces

---

[19] Stephen Biddle, *Military Power: Explaining Victory and Defeat in Modern Battle*, Princeton, N.J.: Princeton University Press, 2004, p. 21.

do. We discuss these influences in more detail in this section, and we out-line our four related indicators in the following section.

Although military inferiority does not necessitate failure in war, leaders should see in their militaries some hope for victory or avoidance of decisive defeat, even if the possibility seems improbable. Liberation movements in colonial countries, such as the United States in the 1770s and Algeria in the 1950s, succeeded in recruiting sufficient numbers of troops and secur-ing enough weapons to make plausible the hopes of victory against militar-ily superior foes. By contrast, militaries that face overwhelming odds are likely to see little point in continuing the fight. In World War II, Belgium and the Netherlands opposed German invasion, but their militaries quickly yielded in the face of overwhelming German military superiority. Research by Paul Huth, a widely respected expert and pioneer in conflict studies at the University of Maryland, suggests that an advantage of between 3:1 and 9:1 may be regarded as overwhelming. In reviewing case studies of past con-flicts, Huth found that weak militaries facing such daunting odds tended to yield rather than fight.[20] For purposes of this study, a ratio of enemy to friendly forces on the battlefield greater than the average of this range, 6:1, is assumed to be overwhelming.

Superior weapons and equipment can help numerically inferior forces defeat larger numbers of enemy troops, especially when those weapons and equipment are wielded by skilled and well-trained troops. During the Korean War, for example, U.S. airpower and artillery inflicted high casu-alty rates on the poorly equipped but more-numerous Chinese adversaries. But this outcome was not exceptional: Scholars have found little correla-tion between (1) the numbers of troops and equipment between sides and (2) battlefield outcomes.[21] Biddle similarly found that militaries equipped with more-advanced, higher-quality weapons and equipment tend to inflict casualties at a higher rate than their worse-equipped enemies.[22]

---

[20] Huth, 1998, p. 114.

[21] Malcolm Gladwell, *David and Goliath: Underdogs, Misfits, and the Art of Battling Giants*, New York: Little, Brown and Company, 2013.

[22] Biddle, 2004, p. 3.

Scholars also have noted that the most-lethal militaries tend to feature highly skilled troops. Biddle has pointed out that better-educated soldiers are easier to train, more adept at operating and maintaining sophisticated weapons and platforms, and more capable of executing complex tasks.[23] The U.S. military accordingly has established education requirements for its recruits. Moreover, considerable evidence has established the importance of rigorous training for superior combat performance. For example, a 1997 Institute for Defense Analyses study identified several training metrics that correlated with performance, such as hours flown for pilots and miles driven for tank operators.[24] Military units that undergo realistic, demanding training that simulates combat conditions tend to fare better in battle than those that do not have similar training.[25] For example, during the Vietnam War, high attrition led the U.S. Navy to found its Navy Fighter Weapons School in 1969, which provided training via a rigorous simulation of air-to-air combat involving well-trained opposition forces. The results were dramatic. Between 1965 and 1967, the Navy's kill:loss ratio against the North Vietnamese (i.e., the number of North Vietnamese aircraft destroyed for each U.S. aircraft destroyed) was 3.7:1 but rose to 13:1 after 1970. During the same period, the Air Force, which had not implemented a similar training program, saw its ratio worsen, prompting it to develop new training methods of its own in subsequent years.[26]

For national militaries equipped with the most-advanced technologies, sustained investment in human capital and relevant public and private-sector organizations and institutions provides a crucial but often overlooked source of military effectiveness. Advanced militaries depend on systems that link weapons and troops to sensors, satellites, and command centers. Only personnel with the appropriate technical and management skills and knowledge are able to assimilate state-of-the-art technologies and

---

[23] Biddle, 2004, p. 13.

[24] Jesse Orlansky, Colin P. Hammon, and Stanley L. Horowitz, *Indicators of Training Readiness*, Alexandria, Va.: Institute for Defense Analyses, March 1997.

[25] Orlansky, Hammon, and Horowitz, 1997.

[26] Benjamin S. Lambeth, *The Transformation of American Air Power*, Ithaca, N.Y.: Cornell University Press, 2000.

integrate them into a cohesive, lethal whole.[27] Other scholars have mined organizational theory to show that bureaucratic misalignment can impede a military's ability to operate as a modern, joint force.[28] Competent management and administrative skills are also required to supply, transport, and support troops in war, as well as to ensure retention, training, and preparation in peacetime. Scientific and academic research institutions provide a foundation for the development of new technologies and the articulation of doctrines based on rigorously derived knowledge.

Integration of these various support elements and military components can ensure the efficient conversion of resources into military power and effectiveness. *Integration* is the organized combination of constituent parts into a functioning whole. In this study, *vertical integration* refers to the organized combination of levels and branches of command in the military to mutually support one another in improving combat-effectiveness. *Horizontal integration* refers to the organized combination of sectors in industry, academia, military, and government to help the military solve problems and improve the lethality of its forces.[29]

In terms of civil-military relations, scholars have noted that highly politicized militaries can disrupt performance through purges, politically driven decisions, the withholding of information, and other forms of interference. Within the Soviet system, for example, political officers interfered with the command authority of officers and attached greater importance to political rather than military qualifications for officer evaluations and promotions.[30] To be sure, highly motivated, ideological militaries featuring rigid political controls can succeed in battle, as the Soviets did in World War II and the Islamic Taliban forces did in Afghanistan in the 1980s. However, these

---

[27] Michael Beckley, "Economic Development and Military Effectiveness," *Journal of Strategic Studies*, Vol. 33, No. 1, 2010.

[28] Roger Cliff, *China's Military Power: Assessing Current and Future Capabilities*, Cambridge, United Kingdom: Cambridge University Press, 2015, p. 178.

[29] Risa Brooks and Elizabeth Stanley, *Creating Military Power: The Sources of Military Effectiveness*, Stanford, Calif.: Stanford University Press, 2007.

[30] Herbert Goldhamer, *Soviet Military Management at the Troop Level*, Santa Monica, Calif.: RAND Corporation, R-1513-PR, 1974; and Alex Alexiev, *Inside the Soviet Army in Afghanistan*, Santa Monica, Calif.: RAND Corporation, R-3627-A, 1988.

forces tend to feature a messianic ideology and fight with tactics that require a lower level of technical skill—tendencies well embodied in the Chinese army of the Mao Zedong era and its "human wave" tactics.[31] Moreover, highly politicized forces tend to fight inefficiently, suffering far larger casualty ratios than more-skilled adversaries.[32] For militaries aspiring to fight in a conventional manner and equipped with technologically advanced weapons, as is the case with both China's and Taiwan's 21st-century militaries, stable relations with political leaders and some degree of professional autonomy on the battlefield are essential.[33] A highly politicized military in which many operational and command decisions are made for nonmilitary reasons is less likely to operate efficiently. For example, if promotions are made on grounds of political reliability as opposed to military competence, the military's leadership likely suffers. By contrast, a military that enjoys relative professional autonomy is better positioned to adapt efficiently to developments on the battlefield and to make operationally sound decisions. Scholars have begun to document how institutions and civil-military relations impair or facilitate the organization and the use of resources.[34] In addition, social and ethnic divisions in society that replicate in the military can erode cohesion and degrade military effectiveness. Within multi-ethnic Soviet units, for example, the troops often spoke several different languages, and Russian was not always a reliable lingua franca. Writers in Soviet military journals complained about the negative effects on solidarity and efficiency caused by poor Russian-language skills among service members who did not speak a Slavic language.[35]

---

[31] Andrew Salmon, "China Honors 'Human Wave' Heroes of Korean War," *Asia Times*, October 24, 2020.

[32] Biddle, 2004.

[33] Risa Brooks, *Political-Military Relations and the Stability of Arab Regimes*, London: Routledge, 1999.

[34] Deborah Avant, "Political Institutions and Military Effectiveness: Contemporary United States and United Kingdom," in Risa A. Brooks and Elizabeth A. Stanley, eds., *Creating Military Power: The Sources of Military Effectiveness*, Stanford, Calif.: Stanford University Press, 2007.

[35] According to Goldhamer (1974, p. 188), in one case, "it turned out that some of the soldiers . . . did not understand the leader's [political] talk. They did not know Russian

In summary, military effectiveness is crucial to ensuring a strong will to fight because, without an effective fighting force, people likely will see little point in continuing a war. And although a military requires a minimum force to be credible, offsetting the numerical advantage of an adversary requires greater lethality. Highly effective militaries tend to feature more weapons, platforms, and troops; better-quality weapons, platforms, and troops; a high degree of integration among the military's services, branches, and administrative bureaucracies and between the military and relevant civilian research and development sectors; and a significant amount of professional autonomy from civilian authorities.

Indicators of Military Effectiveness

This study relies on four indicators to assess a country's military effectiveness (Table 2.2). The indicators related to this variable are assigned a low score of 1 or a high score of 2.

The first indicator is the *quantity of armaments and troops*. In this case, parity is not required; however, the military in question should have sufficient weapons, platforms, and troops to reduce the adversary's military advantage at the point of attack. An adversary with an *overwhelming advantage* (in this report, greater than a 6:1 ratio in armaments and troops at the point of attack, as described earlier) has a much higher chance of success. Absent such extreme cases, however, the relative advantage of an adversary can affect prospects for defense. We assign a low score for this indicator if the quantity of armaments and troops favors the adversary at a ratio between 3:1 to 5:1 at the point of attack. We assign a high score if the quantity of armaments and troops favors the adversary at a ratio of less than 3:1.

The second indicator is the *quality of armaments and troops*. This indicator may be measured first by assessing the sophistication of the weapons and platforms employed by the military compared with those of its adversary. We assign a low score if the country's weapons and platforms are, on average, of lower quality than the adversary's. We assign a high score if the

---

very well." In another instance, a company commander noticed that two privates were shunning their colleagues: "The reason—poor knowledge of the Russian language—[resulted in] fear of saying something wrong and thereby causing the laughter of fellow servicemen. This feeling hampered them in asking questions of the sergeant" (p. 189).

TABLE 2.2

Indicators of Military Effectiveness

Indicator	Explanation	Measurement (high score = 2)
Quantity of armaments and troops	A military must have sufficient forces to at least deny an enemy overwhelming numerical superiority.	Can the defender field sufficient quantities of weapons, platforms, and troops to narrow the adversary's advantage? (High score = The adversary has less than a 3:1 advantage.)
Quality of armaments and troops	Higher-quality weapons and more-skilled troops are generally more lethal.	Does the defender have armaments and troops of comparable quality to the adversary? (High score = The assessed quality of armaments is comparable, and most troops are sufficiently educated and rigorously trained to fight the adversary.)
Organizational integration	Administrative integration enables adaptability and reliability.	Are the military services, command and control, logistics, and civil-military resources integrated to support the vision of warfare? (High score = The assessed level of integration is sufficient to enable efficient and reliable war-related processes and activities.)
Civil-military relations	A military with relative professional autonomy is more flexible than one hamstrung by political interference from civilian authorities.	Do political authorities limit interference to allow militarily sound decisions? (High score = The assessed military commanders are given sufficient autonomy to make decisions according to military necessity.)

quality and technological sophistication of the country's weapons and platforms are roughly comparable to that of the adversary. In addition, this indicator may be measured by assessing the quality of military personnel, based on the education level and rigor of training endured by the military force. Studies have established that well-educated and skilled troops are far more lethal on the battlefield than their less-educated, less-skilled counterparts.[36] Education levels provide an estimate of a soldier's capacity to learn complex tasks. Accordingly, in modern capabilities (such as those maintained

---

[36] Biddle, 2004, p. 13.

by China and Taiwan), a high school education has become the expected norm for enlisted personnel, and a college education has become a widely accepted norm for officers. Studies have also established links between the rigor of military training and performance on the battlefield.[37] Accordingly, we assign a low score for this indicator if the military's average education level is less than a high school degree for enlisted personnel and less than a four-year college degree for officers or if the quality of training is unrealistic and lacking in rigor. We assign a high score if enlisted personnel average at least a high school education, officers have a four-year college degree, and the personnel train in a realistic and rigorous manner. In order for a military to receive a high score for the quality of armaments and troops indicator, both the armaments and the troops must be scored as high.

The third indicator is the degree of *organizational integration* within the military overall, between service branches, and between the military and relevant civilian sectors. This indicator may be measured by assessing the compatibility, efficiency, and reliability among these groups, particularly of their resources, logistics, and support systems. We assign a low score if the country's military has failed to integrate logistics and support services across branches or if the civilian sector has failed to develop services and technologies to support the military in an effective and reliable fashion. We assign a high score if the country's military has successfully integrated its services and if the civilian sector has developed sufficient services and technologies to provide valuable support to military operations, resulting in compatible, efficient, and reliable war-related processes and activities.

The fourth indicator of military effectiveness is *civil-military relations*. This may be measured by assessing the degree to which the administration and operation of the military are carried out according to military necessity as opposed to nonmilitary imperatives, such as political expediency or corruption. We assign a low score if a significant portion of administrative or operational decisions are made for nonmilitary reasons. We assign a high score if such decisions are made primarily for reasons related to military effectiveness and if political expediency and corruption play, at most, a minor role in those decisions.

---

[37] Orlansky, Hammon, and Horowitz, 1997.

Military effectiveness is an important variable in a country's capacity to fight a war. Without an effective military, hope for victory in war becomes unsustainable. We assess this variable as low overall if the total of the individual indicators is 4 or 5, as medium if the total is 6, and as high if the total is 7 or 8.

Variable 3: Durability

Casualties from military personnel in battle represent the most obvious form of costs of war. However, war can cause immense suffering among the civilian populace through other means. As noted earlier, we use the term *durability* to refer to a country's ability to sustain and manage these economic and human costs of war. For instance, despite pretensions to uphold a more surgical form of war by using advanced technologies, modern militaries still unavoidably kill civilians during war. Ballistic missiles and precision-guided bombs might be more precise than other weapons, but they can still pack considerable destructive power. In the War of the Cities between Iran and Iraq in the 1980s, for example, each short-range ballistic missile killed between ten and 20 civilians, on average.[38]

Costs of war can be economic as well. Countries might feel the disruptive effects of war on the economy in the form of scarce commodities, inflation, a decline in the standard of living, and a decline in gross domestic product (GDP). An economy dependent on trade can suffer severe disruption through the effects of a blockade, as the United Kingdom experienced in the early years of World War II. Munitions can destroy factories and other facilities responsible for economic output, and manpower lost to warfighting is yet another cost. In the more extreme examples, a population may experience hunger and exposure to severe heat or cold, especially in harsh climates. Under such conditions, citizens may question whether the war is worth the cost. Fearing such an erosion of support, many national leaders have sought ways to minimize the economic disruptions of war. During World War II, for example, German leaders opted to maintain a plentiful

---

[38] Anthony H. Cordesman and Abraham R. Wagner, *The Lessons of Modern War*, Vol. II: *The Iran-Iraq War*, Boulder, Colo.: Westview Press, 1990, pp. 205–206.

supply of consumer goods to address the concern that erosion in the quality of life for citizens might gradually undermine support for the war.[39]

Hardship from war can also come in the form of damage to infrastructure. For instance, damage to a country's water supply and sewage system could exacerbate problems of disease. And a country highly dependent on energy imports could find its access cut, leading to compounding damage to the economy as manufacturing and transportation stall. Stockpiling can help offset the risk to some degree, but war stocks can also be easy targets for an adversary.

Throughout history, armies have targeted civilian populations as a means of breaking the will of their adversaries. However, the effectiveness of such methods remains debatable. At the start of wars, leaders often pledge to pay any cost to win, and a public that supports such a war might share such a sentiment. Indeed, numerous historical episodes illustrate how inspired leaders can motivate their people to keep fighting despite high costs, as seen in the United Kingdom's tenacious defense in World War II despite losses incurred from German bombers and submarines. Furthermore, scholarly studies of blockades and bombardment have concluded that those methods have generally failed to win wars. Instead, the hardship and damage wrought by such actions have often rallied targeted populations in support of their leaders.[40]

However, the phenomenon of war weariness is also well established. As a conflict drags on and the prospect of victory recedes, mounting casualties and costs from a war can erode public support for the conflict. For example, during the American Revolutionary War, the British public eventually tired of a hugely expensive imperial war and pressured national leaders to quit. The Soviet Union also found support for its war in Afghanistan diminish over time, as did the United States for its war in Vietnam. Even insurgent groups can tire of war. In 2017, the far-left Revolutionary Armed Forces of Colombia laid down its arms after fighting against the government for more than 50 years.

---

[39] Matthew Seligmann, John Davison, and John McDonald, *Daily Life in Hitler's Germany,* New York: MacMillan, 2004, p. 179.

[40] Lance E. Davis and Stanley L. Engerman, *Naval Blockades in Peace and War: An Economic History Since 1750,* New York: Cambridge University Press, 2006, p. 427.

Sensitivity to the costs of war may be especially acute for post-industrial societies in which norms of self-sacrifice have faded. In wealthy, industrial countries, surveys have detected a general decline in the willingness of young people to fight for their country. In 2015, Ronald Inglehart, Bi Puranan, and Christian Welzel noted that increasing prosperity through industrialization has corresponded with dramatic changes in societal values in virtually every country that has undergone such a change. Analyzing public opinion spanning 90 percent of the world's population over three decades, they found that improvements in the existential conditions of a society correlated with an increasing emphasis on ideals of self-realization and a decreasing willingness to sacrifice one's life in war.[41] Studies have shown, moreover, that people in poorer countries are far more inclined to fight wars than those in wealthy countries are.[42]

In conclusion, the impact of various costs of a conflict may be debatable in the early phase, but support for the war could erode over the long term if the costs are high enough. Costs may be measured by the number of military and civilian casualties, as well as by the losses to physical infrastructure, lost revenue from disrupted trade and finance, and physical destruction. People in post-industrial societies might be especially prone to question whether war is worth the cost if the people experience a major decline in their standard of living.

Indicators of Durability

For this variable, we developed three indicators to measure a country's durability (Table 2.3). A higher score for each indicator suggests a higher level of durability and overall lower vulnerability. By contrast, a lower score reflects a higher sensitivity to the costs of war, especially over the longer term. The indicators related to this variable are assigned a low score of 1 or a high score of 2.

---

[41] Ronald Inglehart, Bi Puranen, and Christian Welzel, "Declining Willingness to Fight for One's Country: The Individual-Level Basis of the Long Peace," *Journal of Peace Research*, Vol. 52, No. 4, 2015.

[42] Frances Stewart, "Root Causes of Violent Conflict in Developing Countries," *BMJ*, Vol. 324, No. 7333, December 2002.

TABLE 2.3

Indicators of Durability

Indicator	Explanation	Measurement (high value = 2)
Economy	A country dependent on trade is vulnerable to disruption.	How insulated is the country from disruptions in trade?
		High score = Trade dependency is less than 10%, or the country would likely experience less than a 10% decline in GDP as a result of trade disruption in war.
Infrastructure	Disruption to power production could exacerbate hardships and economic damage.	How insulated is the country from disruptions in energy imports?
		High score = Most of the country's energy supplies are indigenous.
Public resilience	A public's low tolerance for hardship could mean fragile support for a war.	How willing are the people to fight for their country and endure hardship?
		High score = Polls indicate that more than 50% of the population express a willingness to fight for their country and endure hardship.

The first indicator is the durability of the *economy*. For purposes of this study, trade dependence provides a rough estimate of a country's vulnerability to economic disruption. A country's trade dependency is measured by dividing aggregate imports and exports by the GDP over the same period and then multiplying by 100 to get a percentage. Thus, if trade is disrupted, the country's GDP can be expected to suffer in a proportionate manner. As an example, in a country with a 20-percent trade dependency, cessation of all trade would result in a 20-percent drop in GDP. A decline of more than 10 percent in GDP results in an economic depression, which in a modern economy can impose severe hardships that might erode support for war. Accordingly, we assign a low score for durability of the economy if (1) a country has a trade dependency above 10 percent and is vulnerable to a complete cessation of trade or (2) the combined effect of vulnerability to trade disruption and trade dependency could result in a decline in GDP of more than 10 percent during a war. We assign a high score for durability if the country facing the prospect of a complete cessation in inter-state trade has a trade dependency below 10 percent or the country is unlikely to experience a 10-percent or more decline in GDP from disruptions in trade.

The second indicator is the durability of *infrastructure*. Infrastructure involves transportation, water, power, and other systems. However, out of consideration of appropriate weighting for this indicator, we consider only the power system in this analysis. Because of the potential compounding effects of disruption, energy access provides a basic proxy of the state of a country's infrastructure. For example, a loss of access to a large majority or half of a country's energy supplies could affect economic output, transportation, and the generation of electric power to keep people safe and healthy. We assign a low score for this indicator if the country is highly dependent on energy imports. For example, a country that depends on imports for a large majority (e.g., 60 percent) of its energy would be highly vulnerable to disruption because measures to conserve energy use through rationing and other methods would probably not be enough to compensate for the shortfall in supply. We assign a high score for this indicator if the country relies primarily on indigenous or renewable sources of energy. For example, if the country imports only a small minority (e.g., 20 percent) of its energy supplies, it may be able to minimize harm to its economy and the well-being of its people through a combination of conservation and rationing while relying on domestic energy sources.

The third indicator of durability is *public resilience*. This indicator may be measured through polls that survey the attitudes of the people toward war, sacrifice, and potential losses in the standard of living. Studies suggest that people in post-industrial societies show a greater reluctance to endure hardship than those in poorer countries do.[43] Rates of voluntary recruitment into the armed forces can provide a rough gauge of how willing a country's young people are to endure hardship and face danger. In general, post-industrial societies have experienced a decreasing willingness among young people to serve in the armed forces.[44] The more people who express a willingness to endure hardship for national goals, the larger the pool of available military recruits and the potentially larger base of political support for continuing

---

[43] Inglehart, Puranan, and Welzel, 2015, p. 418.

[44] Philip Bump, "Millennials Embrace a Long-Standing Tradition: Letting Someone Else Fight Their Wars," *Washington Post*, December 10, 2015.

a war. By contrast, if the pool of people who express views of resilience is small, national leaders may find support for a war erode quickly and may struggle to find motivated volunteers to serve in the armed forces. Accordingly, we assign a low score for this indicator if polls indicate that less than a large majority (e.g., 60 percent) of the people express a willingness to fight for their country and endure hardship. We assign a high score if polls indicate that more than a large majority of the people express such a willingness.

Strong political leadership and an effective military may overshadow a country's vulnerability to hardship at the onset of war. As costs mount, however, the population may tire of war. But because this is more likely to occur beyond the 90-day period that is the focus of this study, the high score for this variable's indicators is 2, reflecting that this variable has an overall smaller role in the assessment than some of the other variables do. We assess this variable as low overall if the total of the individual indicators is 3 or 4, medium if the total is 5, and high if the total is 6.

Variable 4: Military Intervention by an Ally

Scholars have debated the relationship between alliances and war. Some analysts have concluded that military alliances improve deterrence and reduce the propensity of nations to attack, while other analysts have concluded that alliances embolden countries to start wars.[45] Still other analysts have noted that most wars are bilateral affairs precisely because aggressors tend to attack countries that lack allies and are thus easier to defeat.[46] The specific content of agreements for alliances may matter for the onset of conflict. Agreements that pledge support for offensive attack or non-involvement in attack correlate with conflict more than do the agreements that pledge support only in self-defense situations.[47]

---

[45] Alistair Smith, "Alliance Formation and War," *International Studies Quarterly*, Vol. 39, No. 4, December 1995.

[46] Scott Sigmund Gartner and Randolph M. Siverson, "War Expansion and War Outcome," *Journal of Conflict Resolution*, Vol. 40, No. 1, March 1996.

[47] Brett Ashley Leeds, "Do Alliances Deter Aggression? The Influence of Military Alliances on the Initiation of Militarized Interstate Disputes," *American Journal of Political Science*, Vol. 47, No. 3, July 2003.

Few studies have examined the relationship between alliances and a country's will to fight. In his research, Huth found that, in deterring aggression, alliance ties mattered less than the correlation of forces at the scene of a dispute.[48] However, our review of historical events suggests that military intervention by an ally can play a critical role in sustaining a beleaguered country's war effort. When a targeted country features strong political leaders, a cohesive society, and an effective military, its powerful allies may have more time to consider whether and when to intervene. In 1979, for example, Vietnam successfully repelled a Chinese invasion. Although Hanoi might have been disappointed that its ally, the Soviet Union, failed to provide more-direct support, the Vietnamese military performed sufficiently well that a Soviet intervention was not required.

However, when a targeted country features weak political leaders, a divided and polarized society, and/or a weak or ineffective military, military intervention by an ally might be critical to bolstering the country's capacity to wage war. Moreover, if the weaknesses are grave, the stronger ally may need to intervene earlier and in a robust manner to prevent the total collapse of the besieged country. In 1943, Italy faced an invasion by the Allies. The country featured weak political leadership, a civil war, division among officials, and a polarized society. Moreover, the Italian military remained weak. To cope with the Allied threat, Germany intervened with a large force that eventually grew to 1 million troops. Had Germany failed to intervene so early in the Allied campaign and with such a large force, the Allies likely would have advanced far more quickly through the peninsula. France, too, suffered from political weakness during World War II. French society remained divided and polarized, France's leaders were unpopular, and the French military's performance proved disappointing. Because of low morale, some units panicked and fled the battlefield in haste. A weak and desperate France urgently needed a large and decisive intervention to stay in the war. France's ally, the United Kingdom, intervened early, but the British Expeditionary Force that it provided proved insufficient to the task. Germany defeated France and routed the British force after six weeks of fighting.

In sum, intervention by a militarily powerful ally can play a critical role in not only determining battlefield outcomes but also instilling courage in

---

[48] Huth, 1998, p. 119.

a beleaguered ally. The timing and scale of intervention required to fortify an ally under attack depends partly on the quality of the targeted country's political leadership and the effectiveness of its military. In general, the weaker the country's political leadership and military, the more urgently an intervention by a powerful ally is required to prevent total defeat. The historical cases mentioned in this section suggest that military intervention by an ally can serve as a compensating influence for the military power of the country under attack. Military intervention cannot compensate for weaknesses in political leadership and social cohesion, but it can help strengthen military forces engaged in fighting the adversary.

Indicators of Military Intervention by an Ally

The two indicators for the allied intervention variable (Table 2.4) concern the sense of commitment and adequacy of pledged intervention by the ally, as perceived by the nation under attack. The timeliness of an allied inter-

TABLE 2.4
Indicators of Military Intervention by an Ally

Indicator	Explanation	Measurement (high score = 3)
Allied commitment to intervene, as perceived by the country under attack	Perceptions that the ally is decisive and timely with military intervention can bolster a besieged country's resolve.	From the perspective of the country under attack, how determined does the ally appear to be to committing military forces to fight the adversary? High score = In war, an announcement of commitment appears in a decisive and resolute manner and quickly, such as within 48 hours of the onset of a large-scale attack. In peace, the ally provides consistent, clear, and credible statements of intent to help defend the targeted country.
Adequacy of committed allied forces, as perceived by the country under attack	Perceptions that the ally will commit sufficient force to defeat the attack can bolster a besieged country's resolve.	Does the country under attack perceive that the promised allied military intervention will be adequate to defeat the adversary? High score = In war, the country under attack judges that the ally's promised force will be sufficient to deny the adversary victory. In peace, the ally maintains a credible capacity to intervene in a decisive manner.

vention increases in importance the more vulnerable a country's military is and the weaker its political leaders are. The effect of promised forces for intervention also depends on the disparity between the besieged ally and the attacking force. In this analysis, we judge that the variable of military intervention by an ally has a value roughly equal to that of the military effectiveness of the country under attack. However, because there are fewer indicators for this variable (two) than for military effectiveness (four), a high score here is a 3 instead of a 2 (and a low score is 1). This approach allows the cumulative total of this variable to approximate that of the military effectiveness variable. The allied intervention variable is contingent, obviously, on whether a besieged country has an ally and whether its ally agrees to help. If an ally refuses to commit to an intervention, this variable and its indicators receive a score of 0.

The first indicator is the *allied commitment to intervene, as perceived by the country under attack*. This indicator is easier to evaluate during wartime than during peacetime. The sooner and more urgently the ally commits to defending the besieged country, the greater the likely boost to the country's motivation to fight. We can measure this indicator by assessing the relative timeliness and sense of urgency with which an ally formally commits its military forces to aid the country. We assign a low score if the ally commits its forces in an indecisive manner or after a lengthy delay (e.g., more than 48 hours after the outbreak of hostilities). We assign a high score if the ally declares in a decisive and compelling manner its intent to aid the targeted country and commits its forces quickly. In peacetime, we can roughly estimate this indicator by assessing the supporting ally's statements in support of appropriate defense commitments.[49] We assign a high score if the ally makes consistent, clear, and credible statements of intent to help defend the targeted country, and we assign a low score if the ally's statements are inconstant, unclear, or not credible.

The second indicator is the *adequacy of committed allied forces, as perceived by the country under attack*. To strengthen the besieged country's capacity to fight, that country's leaders must believe that an ally's mili-

---

[49] Michael J. Mazarr, Nathan Beauchamp-Mustafaga, Timothy R. Heath, and Derek Eaton, *What Deters and Why: The State of Deterrence in Korea and the Taiwan Strait*, Santa Monica, Calif.: RAND Corporation, RR-3144-A, 2021.

tary intervention will be of sufficient size and capability to pose a credible hope of defeating the adversary's attack. Because the decision to intervene cannot be fully predicted, this indicator similarly can be evaluated most accurately during wartime. For this indicator, we assign a low score if the besieged country's leaders might reasonably doubt whether the planned intervening force will be sufficient to defeat the adversary's attack. We assign a high score if the besieged country's leaders might reasonably conclude that the planned intervening force may be sufficient to defeat the adversary's attack. In peacetime, we can get a sense of the potential scale of an ally's intervention by considering the military forces available and prepared for such a mission. We assign a high score if the ally appears to have prepared adequate forces to carry out a sufficiently robust intervention, and we assign a low score otherwise.

Military intervention by an ally can help offset weaknesses in military readiness and enhance a country's capacity to wage a conflict. Intervention cannot fully replace the value of a strong military, but it can provide a powerful compensating influence. We assess the allied intervention variable as low overall if the total of the individual indicators is 2 or 3, medium if the total is 4, and high if the total is 5 or 6. A peacetime score can give some general sense of the potential value of the indicators. However, because we cannot know ahead of time whether an ally will intervene, the scores for military intervention matter most in the event of a crisis or conflict. If the ally chooses not to intervene, the overall score for this indicator would be 0.

Comprehensive Assessment

In our analysis, we weighted the proposed indicators of the four variables to reflect their relative importance in determining a country's capacity to defend against a major attack. Of the four variables, the most important is political leadership and social cohesion, so a high score for each of its four indicators is 3. A high score for each of the indicators of military effectiveness and durability is 2. Finally, military intervention by an ally is roughly equivalent to military effectiveness but is of slightly lesser value. Thus, the highest potential overall total for military effectiveness is 8, while the highest potential total for military intervention by an ally is 6. This reflects the

TABLE 2.5

Scoring for Overall Assessments of Each Variable

Variable	Overall Assessment Based on Total Score		
	Low	Medium	High
Political leadership and social cohesion	4–6	7–9	10–12
Military effectiveness	4–5	6	7–8
Durability	3–4	5	6
Military intervention by an ally[a]	2–3	4	5–6
Total capacity to defend against attack[b]	< 16	16–19	> 20

[a] This variable is dependent on the ally choosing to intervene. Thus, if the ally does not do so, the variable receives an overall score of 0.

[b] The values in this row do not consider the fourth variable, which is conditional on an ally intervening. An assessment of a high capacity to defend can be achieved if the political leadership variable is also assessed as high, even if the other variables are lower in value. Conversely, it is numerically impossible to achieve a high score for overall capacity if the first political leadership variable is all low scores.

fact that an ally's military intervention is unlikely to fully compensate for the defending country having a fully prepared and effective military.

Once the scores for each indicator are added together, we (or other analysts using this framework) can conduct a comprehensive assessment of a country's potential capacity to resist a large-scale attack. If the total sum is 15 or less (or 18 or less if an ally intervenes and thus that variable is scored), the country's overall capacity to resist an attack may be judged as low. This means that there is a high risk that the country will fail to effectively sustain a determined resistance to enemy attack for 90 days after the onset of hostilities. If the sum of scores ranges from 16 to 19 (or from 19 to 23 if an ally intervenes), the country's overall capacity to resist an attack may be judged as medium; that is, there is a reasonable likelihood that the country will sustain resistance, but the possibility of failure cannot be discounted. If the sum of scores is higher than 20 (or higher than 24 if an ally intervenes), the country may be judged to have a high capacity to resist an attack. This means that the country is likely to sustain resistance for the duration of the 90-day period from the commencement of hostilities.

Several conclusions may be drawn from the setup of this framework. The scoring values suggest that a country with strong political leadership and adequate military effectiveness should be able to reliably sustain resistance for 90 days, even if the country's long-term durability remains doubtful and the promise of allied military intervention is unclear. The scoring values also suggest that a country with severe political weakness and inadequate military effectiveness will require a speedy and large commitment from an ally if it is to avoid a high risk of failure, regardless of how durable the economy and infrastructure are. In general, the weaker the political leadership and the poorer the military's effectiveness, the more essential it will be for an ally to intervene quickly and at greater scale if rapid failure is to be avoided. Even then, a robust military intervention under such unpromising conditions may not be sufficient to avoid outright defeat.

CHAPTER THREE

Peacetime Assessment of Taiwan's Capacity to Resist a Large-Scale Attack

In this chapter, we apply the framework from Chapter Two to assess Taiwan's capacity to resist a large-scale attack.[1] Because there is no way to predict the circumstances that may give rise to war and how those circumstances could affect each of the variables and their relevant indicators, this assessment cannot be regarded as a prediction of Taiwan's behavior in a conflict. At most, an assessment conducted during peacetime can provide some insight into vulnerabilities that could become major liabilities in the event of conflict. For a more accurate assessment of Taiwan's likely behavior in a conflict, we would have to explicitly state key assumptions regarding the circumstances that made conflict possible and then analyze potential behavior under those assumptions. We explore this type of analysis with some examples in Chapter Four.

Variable 1: Political Leadership and Social Cohesion

Analysis of the current state of Taiwan's political leadership and social cohesion suggests that this could be an area of vulnerability. However, this variable is extremely volatile, and there is a high likelihood that many of the

---

[1] This analysis is based on research conducted mostly in 2017 with some updates in 2021.

indicators included here could change dramatically in the lead-up to and during a conflict.

Public Support for the National Leadership

The score for public support for Taiwan's national leadership is complicated by contradictory evidence regarding popular views of the island's democratic form of government, state of institutions, and particular leaders. Taiwan's democracy is among the world's freest, an achievement about which the population justifiably feels proud.[2] Freedom House, an independent watchdog organization, gave the island an aggregate score of 89 out of 100 in its 2016 index of freedom.[3] The World Bank's 2020 governance index similarly gave Taiwan a rating in the 80s and scored China around the 30s for most scores on issues of accountability, regulatory quality, rule of law, and control of corruption.[4] However, public frustration has grown with the slowing rates of economic growth and dissatisfaction with governance in Taiwan. President Tsai Ing-wen and previous President Ma Ying-jeou have both regularly received support rates below 40 percent.[5] Accordingly, we tentatively score this indicator as low but are aware that this can fluctuate considerably. In particular, public support for the island's national leadership could evolve in unpredictable directions during a crisis. It is not implausible to imagine a leader who gains support by defying coercion from Beijing. On the other hand, an unpopular, weak leader who advances wildly provocative measures despite rejection by the populace could prove extremely vulnerable.

Ability of the National Government to Enforce Loyalty

Like many liberal democracies, Taiwan offers considerable freedom for its people to believe, think, and express themselves. Thus, the island has a gen-

---

[2] Grigorij Mesežnikov, *Democratization and Civil Society Development in Taiwan: Some Lessons for Central Europe*, Bratislava, Slovakia: Institute for Public Affairs, 2013.

[3] Freedom House, *Freedom in the World 2016*, Washington, D.C., 2016, p. 23.

[4] World Bank, "Worldwide Governance Indicators," webpage, undated.

[5] Pengqiao Lu, "Taiwan's Biggest Problems Are at Home: Not Across the Strait," *The Diplomat*, November 17, 2016.

eral disinclination to coerce loyalty to the government. Taiwan no longer maintains a massive network of internal security forces to monitor the sentiments of its people, as it may have in the era of authoritarian rule under the Kuomintang political party. However, the government does still have some ability to enforce the military's obedience. Taiwan's military has a police force that is independent of the service branches and that reports to the supervisory committee of the National Security Bureau of the National Security Council. The military police force is responsible, in part, for ensuring discipline in the military and obedience to civilian authorities.[6] As noted in Chapter Two, this score is mostly relevant in wartime. As a liberal democracy, Taiwan's national government does not attempt to enforce loyalty or control signs of disloyalty in peacetime. The situation could change dramatically during a serious crisis or major war, however. Many democracies—including the United States in the Civil War, World War I, and World War II—have enacted policies to control subversion and minimize political division to ensure a unified war effort. In a severe and protracted crisis, Taiwan's leadership might consider similar measures.

Cohesiveness of the Polity

Although Taiwan does not have severe issues with ethnic or religious division, polls suggest a growing polarization over issues of identity and political affiliation. Of Taiwan's residents polled in 2020, 66 percent identified as Taiwanese, while another 28 percent regarded themselves as both Chinese and Taiwanese.[7] The island's residents might be consolidating in favor of a Taiwan identity, but the democratic politics remain polarized and rancorous. In the national legislature, acute partisan resentments have occasionally erupted into brawls and fistfights and resulted in legislative gridlock.[8] And there are sentiments of intense recrimination and distrust between

---

[6] "President Demands Stricter Discipline for Military Police," *Focus Taiwan*, June 7, 2016.

[7] "Poll: Taiwanese Distance Themselves from Chinese Identity," Associated Press, May 12, 2020.

[8] "Taiwan Lawmakers Brawl as Opposition Assails COVID-19 Policy," Associated Press, September 30, 2021.

the officials and supporters of both the Kuomintang and the Democratic Progressive Party. Polls have noted a deep and polarizing political divide and a weakening of centrist, mainstream forces in the primary political parties.[9] Indeed, a 2016 study by the National Bureau of Asian Research regarded Taiwan's partisan divide as its "biggest weakness" in dealing with constraints imposed by China. The authors argued that the political divide "has undermined the government's ability to set and implement effective policies to deal with Taiwan's precarious situation." They noted the frequent use of grassroots protest movements and problems of frequent gridlock.[10] These governance shortfalls have resulted in insufficient attention to defense spending, the needs of an aging population, government support for research and development, and other pressing issues. Accordingly, we score this indicator as low.

However, similar to the other indicators in this variable, the cohesiveness of the polity could undergo dramatic change in the lead-up to a crisis or conflict. If China persisted in coercing and bullying Taiwan, fear of attack could encourage parties to downplay differences and collaborate to defend the island in a rally-around-the-flag effect. On the other hand, China could use propaganda and political warfare efforts to exploit existing divisions among the people, exacerbating domestic tensions and undermining support for the national leadership. China's military has a well-articulated doctrine on employing psychological, legal, and public opinion efforts—termed the *three warfares*—to undermine an adversary's will to fight.[11]

Compelling Ideology

Like other liberal democracies, Taiwan tends to downplay collective ideals in favor of individual rights and liberty. However, it remains unclear how

---

[9] Cal Clark and Alexander C. Tan, "Political Polarization in Taiwan: A Growing Challenge to Catch-All Parties?" *Journal of Current Chinese Affairs*, Vol. 41, No. 3, 2012.

[10] David Gitter and Robert Sutter, *Taiwan's Strong but Stifled Foundations of National Power*, Seattle, Wash.: National Bureau of Asian Research, NBR Special Report No. 54, January 2016, pp. 2, 4.

[11] Academy of Military Science Military Strategy Department, *Science of Military Strategy* [战略学], Beijing: Military Science Press, December 2013, p. 122.

much the ideal of fighting for the Republic of China inspires the people. The Republic of China theoretically represents the government of China, but this vision lacks credibility. Indeed, a 2020 poll showed that just 13 percent favored the ideal of unification upon which the identity of the Republic of China is based.[12] Thus, it is unclear how committed the people might be to sacrifice for the sake of a government with an ambiguous Republic of China identity. Furthermore, experts have observed signs that Taiwan's military may lack enthusiasm for defending the island. In 2006, Bernard Cole, a military expert at National Defense University, reported that many Taiwan officers believe that their troops are "generally lacking dedication to the service or mission of defending Taiwan."[13] Without clear evidence that a majority of the people embrace a broader ideal or ideology, we score this indicator as low.

However, the compelling ideology indicator remains highly volatile and could change dramatically in the lead-up to conflict. The rise of identity politics, embodied in the 2014 Sunflower Movement and the increasing consolidation of public support for a Taiwan identity, suggests potential for a more popular ideology. In March and April 2014, hundreds of thousands of young Taiwanese engaged in widespread protests, including by occupying the Legislative Yuan in objection to trade agreements that would increase Taiwan's economic dependence on China. The Sunflower Movement was not a unique event but rather a continuation of a series of protests—including the 228 Hand-in-Hand Rally in 2004, the 1025 Demonstration in 2008, the Wild Strawberries Movement in 2008, and the 517 Protest in 2009—that opposed increasing political and economic dependence on China.[14] In 2020, 60 percent of Taiwanese polled opposed closer ties with China, and those identifying solely as Chinese dropped from 26 percent to

---

[12] Huang Tzu-ti, "Poll Shows Highest Ever Support for Taiwan Independence," *Taiwan News*, June 22, 2020.

[13] Bernard Cole, *Taiwan's Security: History and Prospects*, New York: Routledge, 2006, p. 175.

[14] Anson Au, "The Sunflower Movement and the Taiwanese National Identity: Building an Anti-Sinoist Civic Nationalism," *Berkeley Journal of Sociology*, April 27, 2017. Many of these protests are labeled by the date that they occurred (e.g., the 517 protest occurred on May 17).

just 4 percent.[15] As of this analysis, growing support for a Taiwan identity had not resulted in any increase in military enrollment. However, young people's attitudes toward military service could change during a severe crisis. Chinese missteps to coerce or bully Taiwan could crystallize resentment toward China into a stronger resolve by young people to defend a more independent identity.

Assessment

Because we scored each indicator for this variable as low (1), the total overall score for Taiwan's political leadership and social cohesion during peacetime is also scored as low (4), which suggests that this area is a vulnerability. Although the people of Taiwan rightfully take pride in their democratic government and personal freedoms, dissatisfaction with national leaders, governance shortfalls, deepening political polarization, and an ideologically weak foundation of support for the idea of the Republic of China underscore persistent weaknesses. However, many of these indicators could change dramatically in a crisis or conflict, so it is impossible to predict with any certainty how Taiwan's political leadership and social cohesion might play out in a future war.

Variable 2: Military Effectiveness

A review of Taiwan's military suggests that this variable is an area of vulnerability. Although there are opportunities for Taiwan to make improvements, the island's military is unlikely to reverse its growing inferiority compared with China's military. In this section, we review each of the four indicators of military effectiveness.

---

[15] Kat Devlin and Christine Huang, "In Taiwan, Views of Mainland China Mostly Negative," Pew Research Center, May 12, 2020; and "Poll: Taiwanese Distance Themselves from Chinese Identity," 2020.

Quantity of Armaments and Troops

To evaluate Taiwan's military effectiveness, we begin by reviewing its available military resources—that is, its weapons, platforms, and active-duty and reserve force—and comparing them with the resources available to China's military, the People's Liberation Army (PLA). Taiwan's military is numerically inferior to China's in every category of weapons and platforms. According to the U.S. Department of Defense's 2021 report on military and security developments involving the People's Republic of China, China had 416,000 ground forces just in the Taiwan Strait area compared with Taiwan's 88,000 total troops, and China could easily deploy more from its total ground force of 1,040,000 personnel. China had a total of 6,300 tanks versus 800 for Taiwan, and China had 7,000 total artillery pieces compared with Taiwan's 1,100. These ratios average more than 3:1, although China could reach higher ratios by committing forces from units stationed in other parts of the country. As of 2022, China had clear naval superiority as well, with 33 diesel and nuclear attack submarines in its eastern and southern theaters versus two total such submarines for Taiwan. Moreover, China had a total of nine nuclear attack and six ballistic submarines, while Taiwan had none. And China's surface ships far outnumbered Taiwan's, with 24 PLA Navy destroyers in the southern and eastern theaters alone compared with Taiwan's four total destroyers. In addition, China's aircraft advantage was overwhelming: China had 1,900 total fighter aircraft versus 300 for Taiwan, and China had 450 total bombers, while Taiwan had none.[16]

Although Taiwan is outmatched in the quantity of armaments and troops, China lacks the amphibious and air assault lift capacity to transport sufficient ground forces to grant it an overwhelming advantage in its initial assault. Thus, Taiwan has sufficient forces on hand to at least raise the possibility of denying China a quick and easy victory. However, given China's superiority in naval vessels, missiles, ground forces, and aircraft, the possibility is hardly assured. Accordingly, we score this indicator as low. Furthermore, Taiwan is not likely in the near term to reverse the unfavorable ratio in a meaningful way.

---

[16] Office of the Secretary of Defense, 2022, pp. 166–167.

Quality of Armaments and Troops

For modern militaries, quality of forces can matter more than sheer quantity. Taiwan's platforms and weapon systems are among the more modern for militaries in Asia. However, they increasingly lag the armaments of China's military, which has benefited from decades of rapidly expanding defense budgets. Taiwan's aircraft are decades old, while the PLA Air Force fields fourth-generation aircraft and even more-advanced fighters, such as the Chengdu J-20. Taiwan lacks modern submarines and has an aging surface fleet, while China continues to add advanced, quiet diesel submarines, such as the *Yuan* and *Kilo* classes, and nuclear submarines. China also has developed modern warships featuring Aegis-like radar capabilities and long-range missiles.[17]

The Taiwan military's personnel are generally well educated, but much of their training is regarded as not rigorous or combat-realistic, especially for the ground forces. Former RAND Corporation defense expert Michael Chase has also noted lasting recruitment and retention difficulties, leaving the armed forces unable to sustain sufficient numbers of capable, motivated, and devoted personnel.[18] The Taiwan military has struggled to transition to an all-volunteer force, partly because of chronic shortfalls in attracting recruits and spiraling personnel costs associated with the transition.[19] In addition, the noncommissioned officers corps is "universally described by officers of all the services as weak and inadequate" because of their short term of service. And because there is a shortage of experienced and trained personnel, junior officers must perform tasks that should be done by noncommissioned officers.[20] Overall, the quality of Taiwan's armaments compares unfavorably with that of China's, and the quality of personnel scores as roughly equal at best. Accordingly, we score this indicator as low.

---

[17] Office of the Secretary of Defense, *Annual Report to Congress: Military and Security Developments Involving the People's Republic of China 2021*, Washington, D.C.: U.S. Department of Defense, November 3, 2021, p. 161.

[18] Michael Chase, *Taiwan's Security Policy: External Threats and Domestic Politics*, New York: Lynne Rienner Publishing, 2008, p. 126.

[19] Vanessa Molter, "Taiwan's All-Volunteer Force Transition Still a Challenge," *The Diplomat*, August 31, 2019.

[20] Cole, 2006.

Organizational Integration

The Taiwan military has developed a joint staff, but the level of integration throughout the force remains incomplete. The services have made only limited progress in becoming interoperable, and the integration of various weapon systems acquired from different countries remains unclear. The logistics and maintenance system is inadequate for the task of supporting the more advanced platforms, so cannibalization and other symptoms of poor maintenance practices are relatively common.[21] In addition, the research and development sector has made only limited progress in producing the types of technologies needed for national defense, and the Republic of China continues to have a relatively weak doctrinal research capability. Thus, we score the organizational integration indicator as low.

Civil-Military Relations

Although, early in its history, the Republic of China featured political commissars, Taiwan's military long ago abandoned such practices. It does have a military police system designed to oversee the loyalty and discipline of the military, but there is little evidence that this system has resulted in substantial amounts of politicization, corruption, and other civilian meddling in the affairs of the military. Although low morale and the politicization of the military's recruitment and manning remains a problem, corruption in the military generally is low, and most experts regard civil-military relations as satisfactory.[22] Thus, we score the civil-military relations indicator as high.

Assessment

After combining the scores for each indicator, the total overall score for Taiwan's military effectiveness is 5, so we assess the variable overall as low. Taiwan may have sufficient forces to deny China an easy victory if China attempted to invade the island, but Taiwan's military inferiority raises doubts about how long Taiwan could fend off a determined Chinese attack without

---

[21] Cole, 2006.

[22] M. Taylor Fravel, "Towards Civilian Supremacy: Civil-Military Relations in Taiwan's Democratization," *Armed Forces and Society*, Vol. 29, No. 1, 2002.

intervention by the United States. Taiwan's military suffers from quantitative and qualitative inferiority in armaments and troops, as well as inadequate organizational integration. Civil-military relations remain relatively healthy, but the state of Taiwan's military preparation raises concerns about its capacity to resist an attack. Considering the slow growth of the economy, defense budgets are likely to remain constrained for years to come. Although Taiwan can make improvements in integration and in the skills of its military personnel, it is unlikely to reverse the trends favoring a growing PLA advantage. In a crisis or conflict, Taiwan would therefore almost certainly require assistance from an ally to help resist an attack by China.

Variable 3: Durability

Because of its dependence on seaborne trade and imported energy sources, as well as the proximity of its roads, rails, ports, and bridges to Chinese missiles, Taiwan faces major economic and human vulnerabilities. Even the mere threat of war would likely motivate shipping companies to curtail trade to and from the island. How this might affect Taiwan's resolve to fight would depend on the circumstances of the crisis and the other variables discussed in this study. But there is little evidence to suggest that the economic hardships imposed on civilians alone would be sufficient to compel surrender.

Economy

Taiwan's export-dependent economy remains vulnerable to disruption. China was not Taiwan's immediate choice for trade cooperation, but it was the choice of entrepreneurial Taiwanese and Hong Kong businesses that made legal and sometimes extralegal deals to expand Taiwan's presence in China at the end of the 20th century.[23] In the 1990s, cross-Strait trade restrictions were gradually relaxed, and bilateral investment blossomed. These economic conditions helped set the stage for the explosion in trade

---

[23] Michael S. Chase, Kevin L. Pollpeter, and James C. Mulvenon, *Shanghaied? The Economic and Political Implications of the Flow of Information Technology and Investment Across the Taiwan Strait*, Santa Monica, Calif.: RAND Corporation, TR-133, 2004.

between China and Taiwan in the late 1990s and early 2000s. Taiwan substituted its economic dependence on (and latent vulnerabilities to) the United States for an increased economic dependence on China. Growth in Taiwan's economic vulnerabilities to China naturally followed. In 2020, almost 44 percent of Taiwan's exports went to China and Hong Kong.[24] Taiwan's trade dependence ratio was more than 100 percent in 2018.[25]

Potential economic costs from conflict include shortages in food and consumer goods and declines in living standards. In a 2007 journal article, U.S. Navy LT Michael C. Grubb noted that "the global maritime trade industry is not likely to support Taiwan's seaborne trade in the face of a PRC blockade, leaving Taiwan's merchant fleet to meet the island's strategic resupply needs."[26] Taiwan's heavily urbanized population could also suffer enormous casualties in the event of missile strikes. In light of these vulnerabilities, this indicator is scored as low. For more analysis on China's possible tools of economic coercion and Taiwan's options to resist them, see the appendixes to this report.

Infrastructure

Taiwan's energy dependence remains a critical vulnerability. Taiwan now imports more than 99 percent of the energy resources that it either uses to generate electricity or consumes raw. The share of energy from nuclear sources declined from 15.5 percent of Taiwan's total supply in 1999 to 8.4 percent in 2009,[27] and fossil fuels contributed 93 percent of total primary energy supply in 2019.[28] Taiwan's major supplier for petroleum is the

---

[24] Xinhua, "Taiwan's Exports to Mainland Hit New High in 2020," January 9, 2021.

[25] Republic of China Bureau of Foreign Trade, "Taiwan's Foreign Trade Status and Policies," presentation slides, Ministry of Economic Affairs of the Republic of China, July 18, 2019.

[26] Michael C. Grubb, "Merchant Shipping in Chinese Blockade of Taiwan," *Naval War College Review*, Vol. 60, No. 1, Winter 2007, p. 81.

[27] Bryce Wakefield, *Taiwan's Energy Conundrum*, Washington, D.C.: Wilson Center, 2012.

[28] Evan A. Feigenbaum and Jen-Yi Hou, "Overcoming Taiwan's Energy Trilemma," Carnegie Endowment for International Peace, April 27, 2020.

Middle East, which accounted for about 75 percent of Taiwan's total petroleum imports in 2018.[29]

To indicate the stability of a country's energy supply, we look at the *imported energy ratio*, defined as the amount of imported energy divided by the total energy supply. A country with a low imported energy ratio generally depends less on foreign energy, because it owns more indigenous energy resources to satisfy domestic demand. In 2020, Taiwan had one of the world's highest ratios of imported energy (98 percent).[30]

To promote the use of renewable energy, Taiwan's government promulgated the Renewable Energy Development Act in July 2009 with the goal of increasing renewable energy generation capacity to between 6,500 and 10,000 megawatts by 2030. The Tsai administration hopes to end nuclear power production by 2025, however, which would further increase the island's dependence on fossil fuel imports.[31] Taiwan's government plans to have renewable energy provide 20 percent of the island's needs by 2025, but even if this goal is reached, Taiwan would still depend on imported fossil fuels for 80 percent of its energy needs.[32] Thus, we score this indicator as low.

Public Resilience

Taiwan's population numbered roughly 23 million people in 2015, about 60 percent of whom lived in urban areas.[33] As a result of low fertility rates and lengthening average lifespans, the population is aging rapidly. In 2016, the island's workforce began to shrink by 140,000 workers, and in 2026 Tai-

---

[29] Xu Muyu, Jane Chung, Aaron Sheldrick, Nidhi Verma, Wilda Asmarini, Khanh Vu, Enrico Dela Cruz, Shu Zhang, Jessica Jaganathan, Florence Tan, and Gavin Maguire, "Factbox: Asia Region Is Most Dependent on Middle East Crude Oil, LNG Supplies," *Reuters*, January 8, 2020.

[30] Feigenbaum and Hou, 2020.

[31] "Tsai Confident Taiwan Will Phase Out Nuclear Power by 2025," *Focus Taiwan*, March 11, 2017.

[32] Chris Chang, "Taiwan to Boost Renewable Energy to 20% by 2025, Introduce Trillion-Dollar Investment," *Taiwan News*, February 27, 2020.

[33] Republic of China National Statistics Bureau, *General Statistical Analysis Report*, Taipei City, 2010.

wan's general population is expected to decline.[34] Polls indicate that most people in Taiwan, as in other post-industrial societies, are reluctant to risk their standard of living or sacrifice their lives for the nation.[35] However, China's increasing shift toward a post-industrial society raises questions about whether similar trends may affect the young people there.

As noted earlier, the young people of Taiwan and other post-industrial societies appear disinclined to endure the hardships of military service. Because of low enrollments, in 2012, Taiwan cut the mandatory two-year conscription obligation to four months.[36] Despite the stated ambition to transition to an all-volunteer force, recruitment goals for the military rarely have been met. By 2018, the Taiwan military had recruited more than 80 percent of its goal for volunteer troops, but concerns remain widespread about the military's ability to attract volunteers.[37] Thus, we score the public resilience indicator as low. However, as with the political leadership indicators, popular attitudes could change dramatically in the lead-up to a crisis or conflict.

Assessment

After combining the scores for each indicator, the total overall score for Taiwan's durability is a 3, which is low. Some of the vulnerabilities, such as public attitudes regarding the public's willingness to endure hardship, could change during a crisis. However, Taiwan is unlikely to make dramatic gains in reducing vulnerabilities in its trade dependence, dependence on energy imports, and infrastructure in the near future.

---

[34] Tim Ferry, "Rethinking Taiwan's Immigration Policy," *Taiwan Business Topics*, April 16, 2015.

[35] Inglehart, Puranan, and Welzel, 2015.

[36] "Taiwan Cuts Compulsory Military Service to 4 Months," *Taiwan Today*, January 2, 2012.

[37] Yimou Lee, "For Taiwan Youth, Military Service Is a Hard Sell Despite China Tension," Reuters, October 28, 2018.

Variable 4: Military Intervention by an Ally

In peacetime, the United States has upheld, at best, an ambiguous pledge to assist Taiwan in its own self-defense. The U.S. military maintains a credible capability to intervene with substantial military forces based in Japan and throughout the Indo-Pacific theater. U.S. military forces have also carried out military training alongside Taiwan military forces.[38] On the other hand, Taiwan's leadership in peacetime can have little confidence in any U.S. assistance in a conflict because there is no way to know for sure whether U.S. officials will choose to intervene. Because of this uncertainty, we score this variable as a 0. However, this variable could change dramatically depending on the situation that gives rise to a cross-Strait crisis or conflict.

Comprehensive Assessment

Given the precariousness of these variables and their indicators, there is no way to confidently predict how well Taiwan could withstand a major Chinese attack. The details of how the conflict arose and potential developments in Taiwan's domestic politics greatly affect many of the variables that determine Taiwan's capacity to resist. This peacetime comprehensive assessment can provide, at most, an overview of Taiwan's principal vulnerabilities and identify key variables that analysts and decisionmakers should monitor for clues about how Taiwan's national leaders might behave in a war. As noted in the analysis, Taiwan carries significant vulnerabilities in the political leadership and social cohesion, military effectiveness, and durability variables.

Many of the indicators of these variables could change dramatically over time, however. In particular, the political leadership and social cohesion indicators and the public resilience indicator could, in some cases, lead to a robust resolve to defend the island. Other indicators, such as the vulnerabilities to economic disruption and energy supplies, will be difficult to change any time soon. Furthermore, Taiwan's military is unlikely to significantly

---

[38] Gordon Lubold, "U.S. Troops Have Been Deployed in Taiwan for at Least a Year," *Wall Street Journal*, October 7, 2021.

close the gap with China's military in either quantity or quality in the near term, although there is room for improved integration of the armed forces. In most cases, therefore, U.S. pledges to assist Taiwan in its defense will be critical to bolstering the island's determination to resist a Chinese assault for the 90 days posited here as a minimum timeline for the United States to marshal intervening forces.

CHAPTER FOUR

How a Crisis or Conflict Might Affect Taiwan's Capacity to Resist a Large-Scale Attack

As noted in Chapter Three, even though our peacetime assessment of Taiwan's capacity to resist a large-scale attack indicated a low score for all three main variables and a score of 0 for the fourth (military intervention by an ally), that assessment could change dramatically during the lead-up to or in the midst of a crisis or conflict. In particular, a serious cross-Strait crisis and threat of war would probably strengthen the indicators related to political leadership and social cohesion, but the effect would depend on the nature of the situation. In this chapter, we consider how Taiwan and its people might behave during a crisis or conflict and how the different circumstances might affect the island's capacity to resist an attack by China.

The Impact of a Crisis

Wars are typically preceded by long periods of tension punctuated by repeated militarized crises. If Taiwan found itself in a similar period of chronic tension, repeated crises, and failed efforts to resolve disputes peacefully, many of the most-important indicators in our framework likely would change. How much Taiwan's political leadership and social cohesion strengthened or weakened would depend, in part, on developments in Taiwan's domestic politics in the lead-up to a bigger crisis. Over time, for example, demographic trends could favor a consolidation in public sentiment in favor of a Taiwan identity separate from China, and that would provide a ready foundation for public support for the national leadership, cohesiveness of the polity, and a compelling ideology. On the other hand, peacetime trends could also move toward greater polarization, recrimination, and public dissatisfaction with government performance. In the former case, Taiwan's capacity and resolve to fight a war could strengthen, and in the latter case, it could weaken.

The nature of the crisis and how China behaved could drive major changes in the indicators as well. A Beijing perceived as precipitating a crisis through aggressive bullying could encourage greater public support for the national leadership. For example, Chinese intransigence in demands that Taipei adopt gestures toward unification, as rumored in reports of Beijing's mulling of a revised Anti-Secession Law,[1] could fuel anti-China sentiment in Taiwan. A major deterioration in cross-Strait ties could in turn lead to the selection of bold and resolute leaders, investments to improve the durability of the economy and infrastructure, increases in patriotic sentiment and public resilience, and desperate efforts to enhance military preparedness and effectiveness. A growing sense of threat could also mute issues of political polarization and encourage the people to support the national leadership. If the leadership upheld a compelling vision of Taiwan's political identity, the public might rally and show a greater willingness to endure hardship. In short, the development of a serious and protracted crisis in cross-Strait relations likely would result in significant changes in the variables affecting the island's capacity to resist a large-scale attack. Although we cannot predict these responses with certainty, the most plausible outcome is an overall strengthening of the island's resolve and capacity to resist. However, the favorable changes would probably not be sufficient to compensate for Taiwan's serious military disadvantages.

On the other hand, decisions by Taiwan's leadership could precipitate a crisis. In 1996, President Lee Teng-hui ignited a crisis across the Strait with comments that suggested support for an independent Taiwan identity. Although polls indicate that the public is opposed to de jure and other unnecessarily provocative statements of independence, the possibility of a Taiwan-initiated crisis cannot be ruled out. Most likely, in such a situation,

---

[1] Jake Chung, "China Mulling More Conditions for Invasion: Report," *Taipei Times*, February 9, 2017.

the polity would be severely divided between those favoring more-radical statements of independence and those opposed to that position. Rash and impulsive gestures by weak and isolated national leaders may not gain the backing of a majority of the people, but they could have the militant and enthusiastic support of a vocal minority. Facing political weakness, division, and infighting in Taiwan, China could exploit such a crisis by launching a military attack, especially if it judged the likelihood of U.S. intervention to be low.

The Impact of a Conflict

The trends manifested during the crisis period would intensify once conflict began. In a fight featuring a relatively unified public, strong leadership, and a national resolve to enforce loyalty, the capacity to fight could strengthen. However, a Taiwan riven by division, polarization, and weak national leadership could see its resolve erode further under the pressures of war.

Especially in the former case, the strengthening of Taiwan's capacity to resist a large-scale attack could be further bolstered in war if China faces serious setbacks in its attack. Any major contingency would carry high risks for the PLA, given its lack of combat experience and the challenges associated with complex operations, such as large-scale amphibious assault. China has less-risky options available, but they offer far lower prospects for successfully compelling Taiwan's submission. China has four primary means of conducting large-scale attacks: a conventional missile attack, a joint blockade campaign, an amphibious invasion, and extensive information operations. Taiwan's capacity to resist a large-scale attack would be highest in the first and second options and probably lowest in the third, absent U.S. intervention.

Conventional Missile Attack

A conventional missile attack would consist principally of salvos of ballistic and air-launched missiles against military targets with minimal warning.[2]

---

[2] Yu Jixun and Li Tilin, eds., 第二炮兵战役学 [*The Science of Second Artillery Campaigns*], Beijing: PLA Press, March 2004.

These missiles could inflict great havoc on Taiwan's economy and infrastructure, but missile attacks alone are unlikely to compel Taiwan's capitulation. On the contrary, mounting military and civilian casualties from missile bombardment would probably strengthen Taiwan's resolve by increasing the cohesiveness of the polity and public support for the national leadership, following the pattern that has typified efforts to bomb adversaries into submission.[3] Taiwan's military inferiority would matter less here because of the lack of force-on-force engagement. Assuming favorable changes in the crisis phase that signaled a strengthening resolve, Taiwan would have reasonably good prospects for enduring such an assault over the 90-day period, especially if the leaders had reason to hope for U.S. intervention.

Joint Blockade Campaign

A joint blockade campaign could aim to sever Taiwan's economic and military connections with the world through a combination of firepower strikes and intercepting naval vessels.[4] But, as with a conventional missile attack, a joint blockade similarly lacks a clear mechanism to compel Taiwan's capitulation. The effect would probably once again be a hardening of Taiwan sentiment against China, manifested through stronger support for the national leadership and stronger social cohesion. Taiwan's military would probably lose air and maritime superiority, but the open-ended timeline would provide U.S. forces ample opportunity to marshal forces and attack the blockading naval platforms. The prospects for Taiwan's endurance over a 90-day period would be reasonably high in this situation and could be raised further if U.S. leaders signaled a clear determination to intervene.

Amphibious Invasion

An invasion of Taiwan provides the only sure way for China to replace the leadership with a more compliant authority and ensure unification.[5]

---

[3] Pape, 1996.

[4] Zhang Yuliang, ed., 战役学 [*The Science of Campaigns*], 2nd ed., Beijing: National Defense University Press, 2006, p. 292.

[5] Bi Xinglin, ed., 战役理论学习指南 [*Campaign Theory Study Guide*], Beijing: National Defense University Press, 2002, pp. 225–226.

However, despite gains in PLA capability, an opposed amphibious invasion remains a high-risk operation, especially given the PLA's limited amphibious assault capability and lack of combat experience. Moreover, a large-scale amphibious invasion would require considerable mobilization, offering ample warning to the United States and Taiwan. The demanding requirements of this approach and the risk of major war with the United States make this course of action among the riskiest available to China.[6] Assuming favorable changes in the variables that pointed to a strengthening of Taiwan's capacity to fight in the crisis phase, the island's ability to resist invasion for at least 90 days should remain reasonably high for the near term (through 2025), but the prospects could wane over time if China makes advances in readiness, training, and capacity to transport troops for an amphibious assault. Taiwan's military inferiority and the fact that this course of action could compel unification makes U.S. military intervention an essential component of Taiwan's capacity to fight against an amphibious invasion.

Extensive Information Operations

The ruling Chinese Communist Party has a long history of waging political warfare to undermine the will of China's adversaries. As noted in Chapter Two, the PLA continues this tradition with a well-articulated three-warfares doctrine consisting of psychological, legal, and public opinion warfare. Military writings similarly emphasize that, in the informatized war for which the PLA is preparing, the enemy's will remains a primary target.[7] Accordingly, these nonkinetic methods play a prominent role in China's ideals of warfighting.

As China theorists explain, such nonkinetic activities play a key role in "preparing the battlefield" by helping shape international opinion, shore up domestic opinion, and constrain or undermine the adversary.[8] However, scholars continue to debate the effectiveness of misinformation or directed

---

[6] Office of the Secretary of Defense, 2021, p. 117.

[7] Academy of Military Science Military Strategy Department, 2013, p. 122.

[8] Elsa Kania, "The PLA's Latest Strategic Thinking on the Three Warfares," *China Brief*, August 22, 2016.

information. Older studies found propaganda of dubious utility.[9] More-recent studies have observed the surprising success of "fake news" and noted that misinformation is likely to flourish in environments of low trust in institutions and political authorities.[10] These studies suggest that Chinese efforts to undermine the Taiwan military's morale and the public's support for war likely would have greater effect if Taiwan's leadership was weak and unpopular. But the efforts alone would not necessarily compel Taiwan's government to capitulate. Taiwan's leaders and public could be demoralized by PLA information operations yet nevertheless refuse to comply with Beijing's demands. Moreover, Taiwan's government could implement information control measures to counter these actions. The effectiveness of China's information operations would decline even further if Taiwan had strong political leadership and social cohesion.

Although not analyzed in this report, China's own shortcomings should be considered when evaluating Taiwan's capacity to resist a large-scale attack by its neighbor. Despite impressive gains in modernization, the PLA remains untested, and each of its options for compelling Taiwan's submission carry huge risks and disadvantages. For the near term, these drawbacks can partially offset Taiwan's own liabilities, strengthening the island's prospects in a crisis or conflict. However, if the PLA continues to make improvements in preparedness while Taiwan's military languishes, China's advantage could grow.

---

[9] L. John Martin, "The Effectiveness of International Propaganda," *Annals of the American Academy of Political and Social Science*, Vol. 398, No. 1, November 1971.

[10] Carina Storrs, "How Effective Are Misinformation Campaigns to Manipulate Public Opinion?" *Scientific American*, January 18, 2010.

CHAPTER FIVE

Conclusions, Implications, and Recommendations

Our analysis suggests that changes in aspects of Taiwan's political leadership and social cohesion offer the surest path for developing a robust capacity to resist a large-scale attack. This finding raises a conundrum for U.S. decisionmakers. The current Taiwan government adheres to an ambiguous identity regarding China that conforms to official U.S. policy but that appears to inspire little enthusiasm among the public. In a crisis, a government that adheres to that policy might not inspire the popular enthusiasm required to direct a dogged and relentless defense. If the government suffers from compounding problems of social division, political weakness, and poor military effectiveness, then an earlier and more-robust U.S. intervention will be required to minimize the risk of a rapid defeat of Taiwan. However, as U.S. involvements in Vietnam and the 21st-century wars in Afghanistan and Iraq have illustrated, interventions in such inauspicious conditions may result in a war effort that is longer or larger (or both) than initially planned. Those examples also offer little reason to hope for a favorable outcome from such an intervention.

Yet a situation in which Taiwan's resolve to fight is strongest might not align with U.S. policy. For instance, it is not implausible to imagine that intense coercion by China could drive future Taiwan leaders to a path resembling independence. With the right popular leader and articulation of a compelling ideology, the public and military might show a greater willingness to sacrifice for some bold ideal, such as an independent Taiwan. From the point of view of conventional U.S. policy, however, intervention under such conditions could be undesirable. The U.S. government has adhered to the "One China" policy as a means to best protect U.S. interests. Accordingly, U.S. presidents have stated that the government would not support an independent Taiwan.[1] The decision to intervene in a fight between an aggressive China and a defiant Taiwan could prove a wrenching and precarious one for U.S. leaders.

Efforts to focus on improving Taiwan's military effectiveness without addressing the other variables offer little hope of resolving this conundrum. In many ways, an exclusive focus on military preparedness would replicate the U.S. experience with other allied and partner states in which the United States arms and equips a foreign government that is compatible with U.S. interests but suffers political weaknesses. As shown in South Vietnam, Afghanistan, and Iraq, a well-equipped military led by weak national authorities is likely to result in an uneven or disappointing performance in battle.

Table 5.1 illustrates these points by highlighting how variation in the three main variables could affect Taiwan's capacity to withstand a large-scale attack. In the table, we present two hypothetical situations. In the

TABLE 5.1

Variation in the Assessment of Variables in Hypothetical Cases of Taiwan Facing a Large-Scale Attack

Hypothetical Case	Variable 1: Political Leadership and Social Cohesion	Variable 2: Military Effectiveness	Variable 3: Durability	Capacity to Withstand a Large-Scale Attack
Strong leadership and a cohesive society, weak military, economic and infrastructure vulnerabilities	High	Low	Low	High
Weak leadership and a divided society, dramatically improved military, economic and infrastructure vulnerabilities	Low	High	Low	Low

---

[1] "Biden Clarifies Use of 'Independent,'" *Taipei Times*, November 18, 2021.

first case, Taiwan has strong political leadership and a cohesive society. Its military has not experienced substantial improvements from the peacetime status quo, and the vulnerabilities in the economy and infrastructure persist. Nevertheless, because of the outsized importance of the political leadership and social cohesion variable, prospects are favorable for a strong Taiwanese resolve to withstand a major attack. By contrast, in the second hypothetical case, Taiwan has weak leadership and a divided society. Its military has dramatically improved in all dimensions, perhaps owing to consistent and generous assistance by the United States, but these improvements are insufficient to overcome the deficiencies in the other two variables. The result is an unfavorable prospect for Taiwan's capacity to endure the large-scale attack.

Implications

The findings from this study raise several implications for U.S. planners and policymakers. First, for insight into Taiwan's capacity to resist an attack, analysts should pay close attention to the quality and strength of the island's political leadership and the degree of social cohesion in the lead-up to a crisis or conflict. The state of the Taiwan military and the island's enduring vulnerabilities should be regarded as of secondary importance.

Second, Taiwan's disadvantage in the quantity of armaments and troops does not doom it to defeat. Taiwan can take important steps to improve the effectiveness of its military. However, even if Taiwan's military dramatically improves its combat-effectiveness, China's military advantage will likely continue to grow because of China's enormous resource advantage. Given these trends, Taiwan's ability to withstand a major attack by China for the posited 90-day period increasingly will hinge on the strength of its political leadership and social cohesion above all other variables.

Third, the impact of severe casualties and economic loss likely would cut two ways in a major war. Initially, Taiwan's public likely would rally around the national leadership and favor resisting an aggressive China. However, over the long term, heavy costs of conflict likely would erode public support for continuing the war. How public support ultimately changes over time could vary depending on the strength of Taiwan's political leadership and the degree of social cohesion.

Finally, because of Taiwan's military disadvantages and low durability, successfully withstanding a large-scale Chinese attack would require military intervention by the United States. A well-led and socially cohesive Taiwan might be able to mount a determined resistance for a long time, but, without a robust U.S. military intervention, China's enormous advantage in military resources likely would allow it to eventually subjugate the island.

Recommendations

U.S. officials should continue to help Taiwan strengthen its military. Improvements in the quality of platforms and weapons, the skill of the troops, the integration of the force, and the military's professional autonomy could increase the lethality of the force and thereby both bolster the island's confidence in its defenses and help deter China. However, China's deepening military advantage suggests that, even with major improvements to Taiwan's defenses, U.S. intervention will remain necessary to deter or defeat a Chinese attack.

U.S. officials can help Taiwan counter Chinese information operations and economic coercion. Chinese authorities have frequently employed such methods as a low-risk way to advance the country's goals, but these tactics have thus far been met with little success in Taiwan. Taiwan is generally better positioned to counter these non-war tactics, but U.S. support in such efforts will remain important.

Finally, even if Taiwan's political leadership and social cohesion are strong and its military is expected to be effective against China's military, U.S. military intervention would be required for Taiwan to withstand a major attack. The speed, clarity, and credibility of any pledged U.S. military support could be a critical factor in sustaining Taiwan's ability to resist.

Taiwan's Economic Dependence on China

Taiwan has one of the world's largest and most-developed economies, generating approximately $611 billion (in U.S. dollars) in 2019, which was larger than that of many of its regional peers in the Pacific, including Malaysia, Vietnam, and the Philippines. However, that GDP was only one-twentieth the size of China's GDP in 2019, which was around $14 trillion (in U.S. dollars).[1] In this appendix, we review the composition of Taiwan's economy and the island's economic dependence on China, which helps indicate Taiwan's economic durability. The components of Taiwan's GDP—a typical measure for economic strength and the means with which to pursue a national strategy—are consumption, trade (net exports equals exports minus imports), investment, and government expenditure. These components are outlined in Table A.1. Because Taiwan is not considered a country in many statistical accountings, there is some variance in GDP values among Taiwanese, U.S., Chinese, and nongovernmental sources. In the table, we provide data from Taiwanese and U.S. sources for reference.

In evaluating Taiwan's economic dependence and vulnerabilities, we give special consideration to the trade component of Taiwan's GDP, for two reasons:

1. Trade immediately invokes a dependency in government-to-government relations, between a partner or partners in economic

---

[1] Central Intelligence Agency, "The World Factbook: Taiwan," webpage, November 19, 2021a; and Central Intelligence Agency, "The World Factbook: China," webpage, November 30, 2021b.

TABLE A.1

Taiwan's GDP, by Component, 2015

Component of GDP	Reported by Taiwan		Reported by the United States	
	Amount ($U.S. billions)[a]	Percentage of the Economy	Amount ($U.S. billions)	Percentage of the Economy
Consumption	286.4	55.1	275.1	53.0
Trade (net exports)	40.2	7.7	61.2	11.8
Investment	117.8	22.7	109.5	21.1
Government expenditure	75.6	14.5	73.2	14.1
Total GDP	520.1	100.0	519.0	100.0

SOURCE: Central Intelligence Agency, *The CIA World Factbook 2016*, Washington, D.C.: Skyhorse, November 24, 2015.

NOTE: Because of rounding, numbers might not sum exactly.

[a] We converted the amounts at a rate of 30 New Taiwan dollars per one U.S. dollar.

exchange. National security claims can potentially trump any commercial interest, so each trade participant always holds a veto over collaborative commercial activity.

2. Trade has a unique relevance for island economies. Because it lacks any significant natural energy or metal resources, Taiwan is dependent on trade to compensate for the absence of domestic raw materials, and firms must factor logistical considerations into every aspect of their operations.

Taiwan has never enjoyed a diversified trading portfolio. If Taiwan were a stock investor, its portfolio might include just five or six blue-chip stocks and a few other holdings. Taiwan has historically been dependent on just a few countries to achieve its surpluses. Of course, international trade, with complex logistical chains and select export markets, does not neatly conform to portfolio theory. Semiconductors and flat-screen televisions cannot be exported to low-demand markets in developing countries as easily as they can be exported to higher-demand markets in the United States and Europe. The top recipients of Taiwan's exports from 1989 to 2016 are shown in Figure A.1.

China's share of Taiwanese exports was almost nonexistent in 1989, but by the end of 2016, China was easily Taiwan's most significant market.

FIGURE A.1

Taiwan's Top Export Markets, 1989–2016

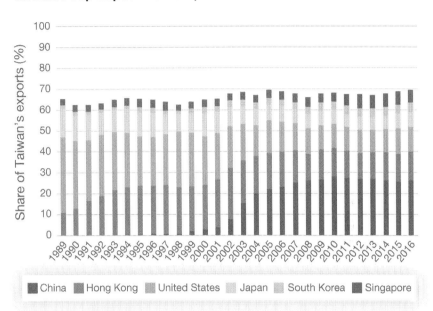

SOURCE: Republic of China Directorate General of Customs Administration, "Trade Statistics," web tool, Bureau of Foreign Trade, November 11, 2021.

This observation is doubly important when we consider how uneven bilateral Taiwan-China trade is. Taiwan's favorable trade ratio with China is the result of three factors:

1. China trade negotiators were tolerant of unequal trade deals with Taiwan to incentivize Taiwan to participate in trade, particularly during periods in which the Kuomintang held majorities in Taiwan's Legislative Yuan. At the same time, Kuomintang politicians were under domestic pressure to limit imports and investment from China as a concession to Taiwanese public criticism that trade could "hollow out" Taiwan's economy.[2]

---

[2]   Robert F. Ash, "Taiwan: Economy," Europa World Plus, London, 2017.

2. China has been reluctant to criticize these terms of trade through the most obvious channel, World Trade Organization arbitration. Even though Taiwan and China are both members of the organization, China is unlikely to utilize these trade channels, because doing so might unintentionally confer nation-state legitimacy to Taiwan.[3]

3. Unbalanced bilateral trade is only one element of the cross-Strait economic relationship. The potential for technology transfer and enhanced tax revenues are two obvious benefits that China accrues by allowing the current terms of trade.

Cross-Strait trade is thus critical to sustaining Taiwan's growth. A 2014 snapshot of Taiwan's net exports with select partners suggests that cross-Strait trade is covering an array of trade deficits that Taiwan incurs from Japan, South Korea, and the European Union trading bloc (Figure A.2).

In less than three decades, Taiwan's economy shifted from being entirely disconnected from China to being dependent on China to sustain positive economic growth in the face of development headwinds.

---

[3] Paul Irwin Crookes and Jan Knoerich, *Cross-Taiwan Strait Relations in an Era of Technological Change: Security, Economic and Cultural Dimensions*, London: Palgrave Macmillan, 2015, p. 105.

FIGURE A.2

Taiwan's Balance of Trade with Select Partners, 2014

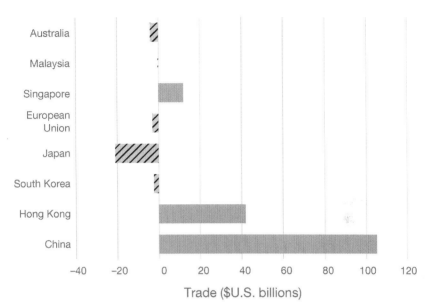

Trade ($U.S. billions)

SOURCE: National Bureau of Statistics of China, 中国统计年鉴 [*China Statistical Yearbook*], Beijing: China Statistics Press, 2015, pp. 11–16; see also Directorate-General of Budget, Accounting and Statistics, *Statistical Yearbook of the Republic of China: 2015*, Taipei City: Chinese Statistical Association, 2016, pp. 99–101.

China's Potential Tools of Economic Coercion

Part of defining what economic coercion is requires explaining what it is not. For instance, economic coercion does not include acts of war, such as blockading seaports, airports, railroads, or other points of commerce through physical means. Additionally, cyber means to incapacitate or degrade a country's economic livelihood are treated as a separate mode of conflict and not as a coercive tool. Although there may be obvious economic objectives and economic collateral damage associated with such actions, use of force to achieve these ends is not considered economic coercion. Likewise, economic policies that offer pure incentives, such as trade subsidies or preferential loans, are not considered. Loans, trade rebates, and tax benefits all constitute part of a broader arm of economic diplomacy that China does employ in cross-Strait relations, but these measures are neither coercive nor likely to induce any sort of crisis that would confine Taiwan's decisionmakers. Coercion in the context of interstate economic relations does imply that one actor, typically a country, delivers one or more of the following: disruption of commerce, threats to disrupt commerce, or implied threats against another actor to achieve an outcome that aligns with the threatening country's interests.[1] The means are economic, but the goals may be political, economic, military, or a combination thereof. In this appendix, we combine elements of stakeholder analysis and GDP decomposition to evaluate Taiwan's economic vulnerabilities.

---

[1] Murray Scot Tanner, *Chinese Economic Coercion Against Taiwan: A Tricky Weapon to Use*, Santa Monica, Calif.: RAND Corporation, MG-507-OSD, 2007.

Taiwan's Stakeholders

China historically has tried to influence or coerce Taiwan's political leaders by gaining influence with various stakeholders in Taiwanese society.[2] Influence is exercised via official government-to-government bodies, such as Taiwan's Mainland Affairs Council and the Taiwan Affairs Office, and through any number of demographic groups that form Taiwanese society. China's preferred target in Taiwanese society has been the Taiwanese business community that benefits from cross-Strait trade and that has extensive professional and personal ties with China.[3] China has not explicitly offered the logic of seeking to influence the business community, but one can infer from past coercive measures that China believes that Taiwan's business community could be compelled to levy pressure on Taiwan's leaders to effect a change and that the business community's imperative is to sustain predictable cross-Strait commerce, even at the expense of diminished sovereignty. Taiwan's business community might be the largest stakeholder group in Beijing's designs, but it is not the only group. Students, academics, trade unions, government employees, and Taiwanese social organizations are also targets for influence.

Taiwan's Gross Domestic Product

Taiwan's leaders have a broader view of coercion and are held responsible for the entire economic performance of Taiwan and all the related fiscal duties, such as paying government pensions, managing the New Taiwan dollar as a stable currency, and sustaining favorable terms of trade. Taiwan's leaders are focused on mitigating risk and vulnerability through pursuing trade diversification (via the New Southbound Policy) and financial hedging (e.g.,

---

[2] Alan D. Romberg, "Cross-Strait Relations: Marking Time," *China Leadership Monitor*, No. 53, Spring 2017.

[3] Shu Keng and Gunter Schubert, "Agents of Taiwan-China Unification? The Political Roles of Taiwanese Business People in the Process of Cross-Strait Integration," *Asian Survey*, Vol. 50, No. 2, March/April 2010.

maintaining large currency reserves and moderating sovereign debt growth through "zero-based" budgetary principles).[4]

Model of Taiwan's Economic Vulnerabilities

We combined the two concepts of Taiwan's economic stakeholders and its GDP to evaluate the island's economic vulnerabilities. The result is the model in Figure B.1, which demonstrates that China could influence components of Taiwan's GDP, with second-order effects on Taiwan's stakeholders. Likewise, China could attempt to economically coerce select stakeholders of Taiwanese society, with possible second-order effects on Taiwan's overall GDP. There can be dynamic interplay between Taiwanese stakeholders and the leadership executing Taiwan's strategy. Because lobbying interaction between leaders and economic stakeholders may or may not be visible, it will not always be possible to state a definitive link between the use of an economic lever and an outcome. Instead, this model offers a framework for considering the many vectors that influence Taiwanese decisionmakers before and during a crisis so that analysts can understand and identify first- and second-order outcomes related to economic coercion.

The bottom left of the figure shows examples of economic coercion tools that China has previously used against Taiwan or other countries or that it could deploy if Beijing thought it necessary. (For more on potential coercive measures, see Table B.1 later in this appendix.) The bottom right of Figure B.1 includes a nonexhaustive list of various stakeholders that China has considered influencing or tried to influence through economic leverage. This simplified model of economic coercion focuses on just two avenues through which Taiwan's leaders could face a crisis:

1. Disruption to core components of the national economy. By influencing and degrading the fundamentals of Taiwan's economic balance sheet, it could be possible to severely erode the capacity of Taiwan's leaders to govern. Basic tasks—such as funding government expenditures for pensions, servicing debt payments, and meeting

---

[4] Republic of China, *2017 Central Government Budget Overview*, Taipei City, 2017, pp. 3–16.

FIGURE B.1

Model of China's Potential Means to Influence Taiwan's Economy

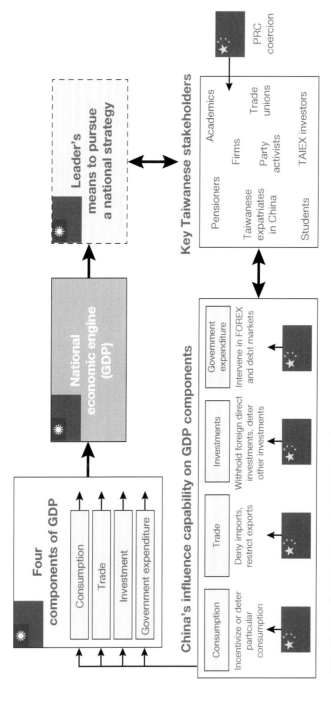

SOURCE: Author illustration informed by Global Agenda Council on Geo-Economics, "The Age of Economic Coercion: How Geo-Politics Is Disrupting Supply Chains, Financial Systems, Energy Markets, Trade and the Internet," World Economic Forum white paper, January 2016.

NOTE: FOREX = foreign exchange; TAIEX = Taiwan Stock Exchange Capitalization Weighted Stock Index.

payroll for the military and civil servants—could all be undermined if sufficient economic disruption occurred. The extent to which any set of coercive actions could generate a crisis depends on not only the strength of the influence measures but also the nature of the countermeasures that Taiwan's government can deploy.

2. Disruption to the livelihoods of key Taiwanese stakeholders. If China threatens or degrades the economic livelihood of one or more groups of Taiwanese stakeholders, the stakeholders might pressure Taiwanese leaders to generate a policy change or concession. For example, if China were to temporarily hold or restrict capital transfers for the estimated 1 million Taiwanese who work or reside in China, it could activate a lobbying force in Taiwanese society that advocates a pro-China agenda.

When making targeted attempts to influence stakeholders or inflict economic pain on an entire economy, no specific outcome is guaranteed. Taiwanese decisionmakers and stakeholders are not billiard balls that China can easily play off one another to achieve political unification. Attempts to coerce Taiwanese decisionmakers have failed in the past, especially in the 1990s, when threats of force from China generated public resentment and enhanced pro-independence sentiment in Taiwan. China's attempts at economic enticement also had unpredictable outcomes, as in the 2014 Taiwanese student demonstrations in response to the Kuomintang's promotion of the Cross-Strait Service Trade Agreement, which was strongly backed by Chinese authorities and media outlets.[5] Instead of predicting an outcome, the model presented in Figure B.1 provides a way to identify the style of coercive measure employed: blunt economic force or targeted coercion. China's coercive strategy could include both types of measures. For instance, following Tsai Ing-wen's election in Taiwan in 2016, Chinese authorities restricted group travel tours to the island, which affected Taiwanese hotel and restaurant operators (stakeholders) and reduced government revenues, threatening about 2 percent of Taiwan's GDP.[6] The boycott was not insig-

---

[5] Keng and Schubert, 2010.

[6] World Travel and Tourism Council, *Travel and Tourism: Economic Impact 2017: Taiwan*, London, 2017, p. 1.

nificant when we consider that Taiwan's economy had been growing by only 2 to 3 percent per year, so a small but sizable disruption without compensating measures (such as a fiscal stimulus) would be sufficient to send Taiwan into an economic recession.

Specific Coercive Measures

Table B.1 provides an overview of the kinds of economic coercion that China has employed or is judged capable of leveraging against Taiwan. In some cases, China has employed the measure against Japan, South Korea, or other countries but not yet against Taiwan. And in other cases, China has not yet tried the measure, but coercion by those means is possible. Examples include speculative currency attacks on FOREX markets (i.e., the selling or buying of a currency on FOREX spot markets for the purpose of manipulating the currency's exchange rate) and rapid debt divestment via sovereign wealth funds.

TABLE B.1
China's Tools of Economic Coercion

Coercive Measure	Principal Aim(s)	Example
Deny commodity imports	• Deny the target export-generated revenue by closing off markets. • Support domestic competitors against those of the target.	Between 2002 and 2008, China imposed punitive import restrictions on nations that supported engagement with Tibetan leaders, leading to an immediate reduction in China-bound exports by an average of 12.5% over the restriction period.[a]
Deny commodity exports	• Withhold exports from the target to prevent value-added manufacturing. • Disrupt the target economy by generating a shortage in critical commodities (e.g., foodstuffs, fuel).	In 2011 and 2012, in response to a Japanese maritime dispute and the Japanese seizure of a Chinese fishing trawler, China restricted exports of rare earth metals.[b]

Table B.1—Continued

Coercive Measure	Principal Aim(s)	Example
Suspend trade delegations	• Deny the target export-generated revenue by closing off high-level dialogue, customs, or other trade officials from performing access-related duties.	From 2010 to 2014, China blocked trade delegations with Norway because of a dispute over the 2010 Nobel Peace Prize being awarded to Chinese democracy dissident Liu Xiaobo.[c]
Boycott brands or national goods	• Deny the target export-generated revenue while still technically leaving all channels of trade open.	In 2012, following a decision by Tokyo's governor to purchase islands in the disputed Senkaku/Diaoyu territory, Chinese authorities tacitly endorsed protests against Japanese firms in more than 200 cities, leading to a substantial decline in quarterly revenue for Japanese firms operating in China.[d]
Encourage mob violence	• Punish the target's associated firms by provoking or permitting physical destruction of capital or other measures that impede business as usual.	In 2017, South Korean firm Lotte had facilities repeatedly attacked by Chinese crowds after the deployment of the Terminal High Altitude Air Defense system in South Korea. Through propaganda channels, the Chinese public was encouraged to demonstrate against Lotte facilities.[e]
Disrupt the stock exchange	• Devalue the target's associated equity markets through threats, disinformation, or divestiture of stocks.	TAIEX market sell-offs occurred multiple times in 1995 and 1999 during Lee Teng-hui's presidency, sometimes precipitated by PLA military exercises and announcements through official media outlets that select Taiwanese firms may be punished.
Disrupt the right to work	• Deny the target's workforce the opportunity to engage in productive activity by limiting or suspending work, visa, and migration permits or implementing worker quotas. • Disrupt the target's economies that are dependent on expatriate workers.	On numerous occasions, Taiwanese business people in China have been harassed, sometimes under accusation of espionage. In 2003, two dozen Taiwanese business people were detained in an apparent response to Taiwanese President Chen Shui-bian's public comments on China's military capabilities.[f]

Table B.1—Continued

Coercive Measure	Principal Aim(s)	Example
Conduct speculative attacks on FOREX markets	• Deny the target a fully convertible currency by devaluing the exchange rate of the target's currency. • Reduce or eliminate the target's FOREX holdings by forcing the target to intervene in currency markets to defend an exchange rate.	No historical examples from China
Nationalize assets	• Destroy the target's capital and investments by nationalizing or threatening to nationalize assets.	No historical examples from China
Encourage sovereign debt divestment	• Raise the target's future cost of borrowing by flooding debt markets with the target's sovereign debt, municipal bonds, or commercial paper. • Precipitate the target's debt default, depending on the structure and term of the debt issuance.	No historical examples from China

[a] Andreas Fuchs and Nils-Hendrik Klann, "Paying a Visit: The Dalai Lama Effect on International Trade," *Journal of International Economics*, Vol. 91, No. 1, September 2013, pp. 169–171.

[b] Global Agenda Council on Geo-Economics, 2016, p. 16.

[c] Benjamin David Baker, "Soul or Salmon? Norway's Chinese Dilemma," *The Diplomat*, May 9, 2014.

[d] Jessica Chen Weiss, *Powerful Patriots: Nationalist Protest in China's Foreign Relations*, New York: Oxford University Press, 2014, p. 189.

[e] Christopher Woody, "China Is Going After S. Korea's Wallet in Their Dispute over the THAAD Missile System," *Business Insider*, March 20, 2017.

[f] Tanner, 2007.

Taiwan's Options for Countering China's Economic Coercion

Taiwan has regularly been the target of China's economic coercion, and several of the island's economic and fiscal policy measures are already shaped to mitigate the impact of potential coercion. This appendix identifies Taiwan's ongoing and potential measures for countering China's economic coercion attempts. The core countermeasures are as follows:

- Pursue a diverse international trade portfolio.
- Maintain fiscal stability.
- Maintain stability in the financial system.
- Maintain stability in monetary policy.
- Cultivate relations with industry and provincial stakeholders in China.

Table C.1 outlines these countermeasures, their principal aims, and examples or rationales.

The purpose of these policy measures is to counter the pain and effectiveness of economic coercion by reducing economic vulnerabilities and dependence. But there is a paradox in employing economic countermeasures: The less dependent Taiwan is on China's economy, the more wealth and potential growth Taiwan's economy forgoes. Certainly, there are other economic destinations for Taiwanese manufacturing, but the most dramatic global economic growth story of the past three decades has been in China. To reduce economic dependence on China is to reduce one's prospects for development. That said, as Southeast Asian nations take larger portions of regional manufacturing capacity, it is possible that, in the decades to come, Taiwan's shift toward other markets may be both a rational economic deci-

TABLE C.1

Taiwan's Options to Counter China's Economic Coercion

Measure	Principal Aim(s)	Example or Rationale
Pursue a diverse international trade portfolio	• Reduce export destination dependence on any one country or combined trading bloc to minimize the effectiveness of unilateral economic sanction.	Taiwan has pursued trade diversification toward Southeast Asian nations in the 1990s and more recently in 2016. The New Southbound Policy initiated by President Tsai seeks to broaden the scope of Taiwan's core export markets beyond Taiwan's few current trading partners.
Maintain fiscal stability	• Limit debt-to-GDP ratios so that interest payments do not outstrip the tax revenue required to service debt (outwardly reflected in high debt ratings and AAA-rated bonds). • Limit sovereign debt issued, or limit debt issued to any one creditor that may have outsized influence.	Because of historically conservative fiscal policies in Taiwan, Taiwan's government holds sufficient economic resources to support stimulus measures in the event of an economic downturn and observes a constitutional limit on debt-to-GDP ratios.[a] Additionally, Taiwan's sovereign debt rating remains low-risk even following the post-2016 election friction with China.[b]
Maintain stability in the financial system	• Prevent short disruption and panic sell-offs in equity markets that could reduce the time that government leaders have available to respond to internal stakeholders and external demands.	Stock exchange "circuit-breakers," "curbs," or mandatory cooling-off periods are a feature of developed exchanges that can minimize fear-induced market activity, providing time for regulators to respond to the impetus of the crisis rather than be preoccupied with the market itself. As of 2017, TAIEX operated a trade circuit-breaker with limits at 10%.[c]
Maintain stability in monetary policy	• Maintain the New Taiwan dollar as a convertible currency on international FOREX markets to ensure that (1) Taiwan's government can service debt and conduct day-to-day operations that require monetary use and (2) Taiwanese firms can conduct foreign trade that is dependent on currency exchange.	Speculative attacks on a particular currency can be combated through a procedure known as currency sterilization. The monetary policy typically requires the central bank of the nation being pressured to utilize its FOREX holdings to reassure FOREX markets that the currency remains convertible at some targeted level. In 2021, Taiwan held the world's fifth-largest FOREX reserves.[d]

Table C.1—Continued

Measure	Principal Aim(s)	Example or Rationale
Cultivate relations with industry and provincial stakeholders in China	• Encourage Taiwanese businesses and citizens to cooperate with provincial and city stakeholders in China in order to maintain a low profile and be a difficult target for any sanctions—particularly boycotts or firm harassment similar to the 2012 anti-Japan protests or the 2017 anti–South Korea protests.[d]	Taiwanese firms in China already share many linguistic and cultural commonalities with Chinese stakeholders, putting Taiwanese firms in a very different set of circumstances than firms from some other countries. When Taiwanese businesses can cobrand products, conduct joint ventures, and cooperate with local Chinese partners, it diminishes the target presented to the Chinese government looking to punish Taiwanese firms and citizens.

[a] Economic Intelligence Unit, *Taiwan: Country Report*, London, 2017, p. 6.

[b] As of July 2017, Moody's credit rating agency scored Taiwan's sovereign debt as AAA—its highest level and higher than many renminbi-issued debts (Moody's Investors Service, "Taiwan's High Income Levels Support the Credit Profile; Geopolitical Tensions, Narrow Export Base Pose Key Challenges," July 17, 2017).

[c] Shinya Abe, "Bourse to Introduce 'Circuit Breaker' in 2016," *Nikkei Asia*, June 12, 2015.

[d] Pan Tzu-yu and Frances Huang, "Taiwan's Forex Reserves Hit New High at End of September," *Focus Taiwan*, October 5, 2021.

[e] Weiss, 2014; Woody, 2017.

sion and a politically important development that reduces Taiwan's dependence on China.

In some cases, Taiwan's freedom to maneuver economically is also constrained by its relationship with other trade partners, such as Japan and the United States. As an example, in 2017, numerous Taiwanese insurers suffered substantial financial losses because of shifts in the New Taiwan dollar that could have been corrected with intervention, but, because of fear regarding U.S. trade retaliation, Taiwan chose not to intervene.[1] Taiwan does have available countermeasures to deploy against China's coercion (Table C.1), but those actions will not occur in a vacuum, and the policy of other relevant actors must be taken into account. Complementary policy by Taiwan's other trade partners would certainly enhance the ability of Taiwan to resist China's economic coercion.

---

[1] Faith Hung, "Taiwan Sits Out FOREX Intervention to Duck Trump Blast," Reuters, March 1, 2017.

References

Abe, Shinya, "Bourse to Introduce 'Circuit Breaker' in 2016," *Nikkei Asian Review*, June 12, 2015.

Academy of Military Science Military Strategy Department, *Science of Military Strategy* [战略学], Beijing: Military Science Press, December 2013.

Alexiev, Alex, *Inside the Soviet Army in Afghanistan*, Santa Monica, Calif.: RAND Corporation, R-3627-A, 1988. As of August 4, 2021:
https://www.rand.org/pubs/reports/R3627.html

Ash, Robert F., "Taiwan: Economy," Europa World Plus, London, 2017. As of May 25, 2021:
http://www.europaworld.com/entry/tw.ec

Au, Anson, "The Sunflower Movement and the Taiwanese National Identity: Building an Anti-Sinoist Civic Nationalism," *Berkeley Journal of Sociology*, April 27, 2017.

Avant, Deborah, "Political Institutions and Military Effectiveness: Contemporary United States and United Kingdom," in Risa A. Brooks and Elizabeth A. Stanley, eds., *Creating Military Power: The Sources of Military Effectiveness*, Stanford, Calif.: Stanford University Press, 2007.

Baker, Benjamin David, "Soul or Salmon? Norway's Chinese Dilemma," *The Diplomat*, May 9, 2014.

Baum, Matthew A., and Samuel Kernell, "Economic Class and Popular Support for Franklin Roosevelt in War and Peace," *Public Opinion Quarterly*, Vol. 65, No. 2, 2001, pp. 198–229.

Beckley, Michael, "Economic Development and Military Effectiveness," *Journal of Strategic Studies*, Vol. 33, No. 1, 2010, pp. 43–79.

Bennett, W. Lance, and David L. Paletz, eds., *Taken by Storm: The Media, Public Opinion, and U.S. Foreign Policy in the Gulf War*, Chicago, Ill.: University of Chicago Press, 1994.

Berinsky, Adam J., "Assuming the Costs of War: Events, Elites, and American Public Support for Military Conflict," *Journal of Politics*, Vol. 69, No. 4, November 2007, pp. 975–997.

Berinsky, Adam J., and James N. Druckman, "Public Opinion Research and Support for the Iraq War," *Public Opinion Quarterly*, Vol. 71, No.1, Spring 2007, pp. 126–141.

Bi Xinglin, ed., 战役理论学习指南 [*Campaign Theory Study Guide*], Beijing: National Defense University Press, 2002.

Biddle, Stephen, *Military Power: Explaining Victory and Defeat in Modern Battle*, Princeton, N.J.: Princeton University Press, 2004.

"Biden Clarifies Use of 'Independent,'" *Taipei Times*, November 18, 2021.

Brooks, Risa, *Political-Military Relations and the Stability of Arab Regimes*, London: Routledge, 1999.

Brooks, Risa, and Elizabeth Stanley, *Creating Military Power: The Sources of Military Effectiveness*, Stanford, Calif.: Stanford University Press, 2007.

Bump, Philip, "Millennials Embrace a Long-Standing Tradition: Letting Someone Else Fight Their Wars," *Washington Post*, December 10, 2015.

Castillo, Jasen J., *Endurance and War: The National Sources of Military Cohesion*, Stanford, Calif.: Stanford University Press, 2014.

Central Intelligence Agency, *The CIA World Factbook 2016*, Washington, D.C.: Skyhorse, November 24, 2015.

———, "The World Factbook: Taiwan," webpage, November 19, 2021a. As of December 2, 2021:
https://www.cia.gov/the-world-factbook/countries/taiwan

———, "The World Factbook: China," webpage, November 30, 2021b. As of December 2, 2021:
https://www.cia.gov/the-world-factbook/countries/china/#economy

Chang, Chris, "Taiwan to Boost Renewable Energy to 20% by 2025, Introduce Trillion-Dollar Investment," *Taiwan News*, February 27, 2020.

Chang, Rich, Lo Tien-pin, and Jake Chung, "Taiwan Would Not Survive Month of Attack, NSB Says," *Taipei Times*, March 11, 2014.

Chase, Michael, *Taiwan's Security Policy: External Threats and Domestic Politics*, New York: Lynne Rienner Publishing, 2008.

Chase, Michael S., Kevin L. Pollpeter, and James C. Mulvenon, *Shanghaied? The Economic and Political Implications of the Flow of Information Technology and Investment Across the Taiwan Strait*, Santa Monica, Calif.: RAND Corporation, TR-133, 2004. As of August 22, 2021:
https://www.rand.org/pubs/technical_reports/TR133.html

Chung, Jake, "China Mulling More Conditions for Invasion: Report," *Taipei Times*, February 9, 2017.

Clark, Cal, and Alexander C. Tan, "Political Polarization in Taiwan: A Growing Challenge to Catch-All Parties?" *Journal of Current Chinese Affairs*, Vol. 41, No. 3, 2012, pp. 7–31.

Cliff, Roger, *China's Military Power: Assessing Current and Future Capabilities*, Cambridge, United Kingdom: Cambridge University Press, 2015.

Cole, Bernard, *Taiwan's Security: History and Prospects*, New York: Routledge, 2006.

Cordesman, Anthony H., and Abraham R. Wagner, *The Lessons of Modern War*, Vol. II: *The Iran-Iraq War*, Boulder, Colo.: Westview Press, 1990.

Costalli, Stephano, and Andrea Ruggeri, "Indignation, Ideologies, and Armed Mobilization: Civil War in Italy, 1943–45," *International Security*, Vol. 40, No. 2, Fall 2015, pp. 119–157.

Crookes, Paul Irwin, and Jan Knoerich, eds., *Cross-Taiwan Strait Relations in an Era of Technological Change: Security, Economic and Cultural Dimensions*, London: Palgrave Macmillan, 2015.

Davis, Lance E., and Stanley L. Engerman, *Naval Blockades in Peace and War: An Economic History Since 1750*, New York: Cambridge University Press, 2006.

Devlin, Kat, and Christine Huang, "In Taiwan, Views of Mainland China Mostly Negative," Pew Research Center, May 12, 2020.

Directorate-General of Budget, Accounting and Statistics, *Statistical Yearbook of the Republic of China: 2015*, Taipei City: Chinese Statistical Association, 2016.

Dykman, J. T., "The Soviet Experience in World War Two," Eisenhower Institute at Gettysburg College, undated.

Economic Intelligence Unit, *Taiwan: Country Report*, London, 2017.

Feigenbaum, Evan A., and Jen-Yi Hou, "Overcoming Taiwan's Energy Trilemma," Carnegie Endowment for International Peace, April 27, 2020.

Ferry, Tim, "Rethinking Taiwan's Immigration Policy," *Taiwan Business Topics*, April 16, 2015.

Fravel, M. Taylor, "Towards Civilian Supremacy: Civil-Military Relations in Taiwan's Democratization," *Armed Forces and Society*, Vol. 29, No. 1, 2002, pp. 57–84.

Freedom House, *Freedom in the World 2016*, Washington, D.C., 2016.

Fuchs, Andreas, and Nils-Hendrik Klann, "Paying a Visit: The Dalai Lama Effect on International Trade," *Journal of International Economics*, Vol. 91, No. 1, September 2013, pp. 164–177.

Gartner, Scott Sigmund, and Randolph M. Siverson, "War Expansion and War Outcome," *Journal of Conflict Resolution*, Vol. 40, No. 1, March 1996, pp. 4–15.

Gitter, David, and Robert Sutter, *Taiwan's Strong but Stifled Foundations of National Power*, Seattle, Wash.: National Bureau of Asian Research, NBR Special Report No. 54, January 2016.

Gladwell, Malcolm, *David and Goliath: Underdogs, Misfits, and the Art of Battling Giants*, New York: Little, Brown and Company, 2013.

Global Agenda Council on Geo-Economics, "The Age of Economic Coercion: How Geo-Politics Is Disrupting Supply Chains, Financial Systems, Energy Markets, Trade and the Internet," World Economic Forum white paper, January 2016.

Gold, Michael, and Ben Blanchard, "Taiwan Says China Could Launch Successful Invasion by 2020," Reuters, October 9, 2013.

Goldhamer, Herbert, *Soviet Military Management at the Troop Level*, Santa Monica, Calif.: RAND Corporation, R-1513-PR, 1974. As of August 14, 2021: https://www.rand.org/pubs/reports/R1513.html

Grubb, Michael C., "Merchant Shipping in Chinese Blockade of Taiwan," *Naval War College Review*, Vol. 60, No. 1, Winter 2007, pp. 81–102.

Huang Tzu-ti, "Poll Shows Highest Ever Support for Taiwan Independence," *Taiwan News*, June 22, 2020.

Hung, Faith, "Taiwan Sits Out FOREX Intervention to Duck Trump Blast," Reuters, March 1, 2017.

Huth, Paul K., *Standing Your Ground: Territorial Disputes and International Conflict*, Ann Arbor, Mich.: University of Michigan Press, 1998.

Inglehart, Ronald, Bi Puranan, and Christian Welzel, "Declining Willingness to Fight for One's Country: The Individual-Level Basis of the Long Peace," *Journal of Peace Research*, Vol. 52, No. 4, 2015, pp. 418–434.

Kania, Elsa, "The PLA's Latest Strategic Thinking on the Three Warfares," *China Brief*, August 22, 2016.

Keng, Shu, and Gunter Schubert, "Agents of Taiwan-China Unification? The Political Roles of Taiwanese Business People in the Process of Cross-Strait Integration," *Asian Survey*, Vol. 50, No. 2, March/April 2010, pp. 287–310.

Lambeth, Benjamin S., *The Transformation of American Air Power*, Ithaca, N.Y.: Cornell University Press, 2000.

Lee, Yimou, "For Taiwan Youth, Military Service Remains a Hard Sell Despite Tensions with China," Reuters, October 28, 2018.

Leeds, Brett Ashley, "Do Alliances Deter Aggression? The Influence of Military Alliances on the Initiation of Militarized Interstate Disputes," *American Journal of Political Science*, Vol. 47, No. 3, July 2003, pp. 427–439.

Lu, Pengqiao, "Taiwan's Biggest Problems Are at Home: Not Across the Strait," *The Diplomat*, November 17, 2016.

Lubold, Gordon, "U.S. Troops Have Been Deployed in Taiwan for at Least a Year," *Wall Street Journal*, October 7, 2021.

Martin, L. John, "The Effectiveness of International Propaganda," *Annals of the American Academy of Political and Social Science*, Vol. 398, No. 1, November 1971, pp. 61–70.

Mason, M. Chris, "Strategic Insights: The Will to Fight," Strategic Studies Institute, U.S. Army War College, September 11, 2015.

Mazarr, Michael J., Nathan Beauchamp-Mustafaga, Timothy R. Heath, and Derek Eaton, *What Deters and Why: The State of Deterrence in Korea and the Taiwan Strait*, Santa Monica, Calif.: RAND Corporation, RR-3144-A, 2021. As of December 2, 2021:
https://www.rand.org/pubs/research_reports/RR3144.html

Mesežnikov, Grigorij, *Democratization and Civil Society Development in Taiwan: Some Lessons for Central Europe*, Bratislava, Slovakia: Institute for Public Affairs, 2013.

Mizokami, Kyle, "How Taiwan Would Defend Against a Chinese Attack," USNI News, March 26, 2014.

Molter, Vanessa, "Taiwan's All-Volunteer Force Transition Still a Challenge," *The Diplomat*, August 31, 2019.

Moody's Investors Service, "Taiwan's High Income Levels Support the Credit Profile; Geopolitical Tensions, Narrow Export Base Pose Key Challenges," July 17, 2017.

National Bureau of Statistics of China, 中国统计年鉴 [*China Statistical Yearbook*], Beijing: China Statistics Press, 2015.

Office of the Secretary of Defense, *Annual Report to Congress: Military and Security Developments Involving the People's Republic of China 2021*, Washington, D.C.: U.S. Department of Defense, November 3, 2021.

———, *Annual Report to Congress: Military and Security Developments Involving the People's Republic of China 2022*, Washington, D.C.: U.S. Department of Defense, November 29, 2022.

Orlansky, Jesse, Colin P. Hammon, and Stanley A. Horowitz, *Indicators of Training Readiness*, Alexandria, Va.: Institute for Defense Analyses, March 1997.

Pan Tzu-yu and Frances Huang, "Taiwan's Forex Reserves Hit New High at End of September," *Focus Taiwan*, October 5, 2021.

Pape, Robert A., *Bombing to Win: Air Power and Coercion in War*, Ithaca, N.Y.: Cornell University Press, 1996.

Pew Research Center, "Public Attitudes Toward the War in Iraq: 2003–2008," March 19, 2008.

"Poll: Taiwanese Distance Themselves from Chinese Identity," Associated Press, May 12, 2020.

"President Demands Stricter Discipline for Military Police," *Focus Taiwan*, June 7, 2016.

Republic of China, *2017 Central Government Budget Overview*, Taipei City, 2017. As of June 15, 2021:
http://eng.dgbas.gov.tw/public/Attachment/7217104714ZX60WRZE.pdf

Republic of China Bureau of Foreign Trade, "Taiwan's Foreign Trade Status and Policies," presentation slides, Ministry of Economic Affairs of the Republic of China, July 18, 2019. As of December 2, 2021:
https://www.roc-taiwan.org/uploads/sites/28/2019/09/
Taiwan's-Foreign-Trade-Status-and-Policies_-2.pdf

Republic of China Directorate General of Customs Administration, "Trade Statistics," web tool, Bureau of Foreign Trade, November 11, 2021. As of December 2, 2021:
https://cuswebo.trade.gov.tw/FSCE000F/FSCE000F

Republic of China National Statistics Bureau, *General Statistical Analysis Report*, Taipei City, 2010. As of December 2, 2021:
https://eng.stat.gov.tw/public/Data/7113143851PNHSNJPU.pdf

Romberg, Alan D., "Cross-Strait Relations: Marking Time," *China Leadership Monitor*, No. 53, Spring 2017.

Rosen, Stephen Peter, *Societies and Military Power: India and Its Armies*, Ithaca, N.Y.: Cornell University Press, 1996.

Salmon, Andrew, "China Honors 'Human Wave' Heroes of Korean War," *Asia Times*, October 24, 2020.

Seligmann, Matthew, John Davison, and John McDonald, *Daily Life in Hitler's Germany*, New York: MacMillan, 2004.

Shih Hsiu-chuan, "Taiwan Could Withstand Attack for One Month: Yen," *Taipei Times*, March 7, 2014.

Smith, Alistair, "Alliance Formation and War," *International Studies Quarterly*, Vol. 39, No. 4, December 1995, pp. 405–425.

Spector, Ronald H., *Advice and Support: The Early Years, 1941–1960*, Stockton, Calif.: University Press of the Pacific, 2005.

Starr, Barbara, "Carter: Iraqis Showed 'No Will to Fight' in Ramadi," CNN, May 24, 2015.

Stewart, Frances, "Root Causes of Violent Conflict in Developing Countries," *BMJ*, Vol. 324, No. 7333, December 2002, pp. 342–345.

Storrs, Carina, "How Effective Are Misinformation Campaigns to Manipulate Public Opinion?" *Scientific American*, January 18, 2010.

"Taiwan Cuts Compulsory Military Service to 4 Months," *Taiwan Today*, January 2, 2012.

"Taiwan Lawmakers Brawl as Opposition Assails COVID-19 Policy," Associated Press, September 30, 2021.

Tanner, Murray Scot, *Chinese Economic Coercion Against Taiwan: A Tricky Weapon to Use*, Santa Monica, Calif.: RAND Corporation, MG-507-OSD, 2007. As of August 31, 2021:
https://www.rand.org/pubs/monographs/MG507.html

Thim, Michael, "Can China Take Over Taiwan by Force?" *Thinking Taiwan*, January 21, 2015.

"Tsai Confident Taiwan Will Phase Out Nuclear Power by 2025," *Focus Taiwan*, March 11, 2017.

Wakefield, Bryce, *Taiwan's Energy Conundrum*, Washington, D.C.: Wilson Center, 2012.

Weiss, Jessica Chen, *Powerful Patriots: Nationalist Protest in China's Foreign Relations*, New York: Oxford University Press, 2014.

Woody, Christopher, "China Is Going After S. Korea's Wallet in Their Dispute over the THAAD Missile System," *Business Insider*, March 20, 2017.

World Bank, "Worldwide Governance Indicators," webpage, undated. As of August 15, 2021:
http://info.worldbank.org/governance/wgi/index.aspx#reports

World Travel and Tourism Council, *Travel and Tourism Economic Impact 2017: Taiwan*, London, 2017.

Xinhua, "台湾新兵娇生惯养体能训练标准被迫一降再降" ["Training Standards for Spoiled Taiwan Recruits Decline Again and Again"], March 23, 2007. As of August 14, 2017:
http://news.xinhuanet.com/mil/2007-03/23/content_5884699.htm

Xinhua, "Taiwan's Exports to Mainland Hit New High in 2020," January 9, 2021.

Xu Muyu, Jane Chung, Aaron Sheldrick, Nidhi Verma, Wilda Asmarini, Khanh Vu, Enrico Dela Cruz, Shu Zhang, Jessica Jaganathan, Florence Tan, and Gavin Maguire, "Factbox: Asia Region is Most Dependent on Middle East Crude Oil, LNG Supplies," Reuters, January 8, 2020.

Yu Jixun and Li Tilin, eds., 第二炮兵战役学 [*The Science of Second Artillery Campaigns*], Beijing: PLA Press, March 2004.

Zhang Yuliang, ed., 战役学 [*The Science of Campaigns*], 2nd ed., Beijing: National Defense University Press, 2006.